PRAISE FOR *TOGETHER*

You never expect to read a book on marriage advice and get so drawn into the stories that you want to stay up all night reading it. Yet that is exactly what happened to me when I read *Together*! Between the stories, the experienced advice from Bill, and the biblical foundation, *Together* is a must-read for anyone who's married or engaged.

Lara Helmling, The Jesus Files Podcast

This book walks and talks with anyone who has a heartbeat for a healthy marriage, regardless of the mess. The author peels back the blinds and uses courageous honesty in telling the story of his marriage to Lisa. I have known the author in the before, during, and present of his story. In reading the book, you will not feel preached at, but oddly encouraged.

Ross DeMerchant, Speaker, Author of *26 Letters*

This is the entrepreneurial men's guide to a rich, fulfilling marriage. If you're struggling in your marriage, or you sense it should be better, read this book! And then incorporate at least a few of the author's suggestions. In Together, Bill McConnell shares openly about how and why his marriage almost ended after 7 years and the steps he took to restore it to a level they could never have imagined. Bill doesn't simply offer theories. Instead he gives practical actions men can take to woo their wives and convince them they are loved. Bill's conversational, pointed and often humorous writing offers no-excuses-allowed advice to help entrepreneurs restore and elevate their marriages.

Julie Sunne, Author, JulieSunne.com

So many marriages today are falling apart. What's often most needed is some practical, "been there, done that" wisdom to help chart a different course. Bill McConnell's book Together does that. In a very readable, authentic style, Bill shares openly from his own life and marriage, offering lots of practical ideas for how you can help make your marriage better.

Alan Kraft,
Lead Pastor Christ Community Church, Greeley CO
Author of *More* and *Good News For Those Trying Harder*

TOGETHER

SURPRISINGLY SIMPLE SECRETS FOR LOVING YOUR WIFE FOREVER

BILL MCCONNELL

Printed in the United States of America

Pulbished by Author Academy Elite
P.O. Box 43 Powell OH 43035

www.AuthorAcademyElite.com

Paperback ISBN: 978-1-64085-524-3

Hardback ISBN: 978-1-64085-525-0

Library of Congress Control Number: 2018968458

Cover Photo by David Dougherty Epic Images

DEDICATION

Umm . . . Let me think for a minute . . .
My amazingly gorgeous and godly wife,
Lisa.
I love you more with each passing day.
Sappy, but, oh so true.

Also, my daughter Shelby,
who told me years ago to start writing books.
OK, you win. I'm writing books.

I love you both.

TABLE OF CONTENTS

ACKNOWLEDGMENTS

In my first attempt at writing a book, I did it all by myself. Writing, self-publishing, the whole shebang. My accountant was so gracious to buy a copy and read it. (Many books are bought and never read.) His first comment to me was, "Have you ever heard of spellcheck?" Ouch. He was right, but ouch. When I thought about it, if an accountant misplaces of one decimal point, someone may owe someone else a lot of money. I appreciated his attention to detail comment because for me it means creating a better book and reading experience.

With this new book, proper proofreading, editing and formatting has been done. My wife is thrilled that the content reflects our marriage in the best of ways. I have made the effort to take care of the little things that mean a lot.

Shhhhh… that may or may not be one of the secrets.

UNOFFICIAL DISCLAIMER

So, I'm a guy. I'm a husband who almost lost his wife due to general stupidity. A husband who learned how to have his wife fall in love with him all over again. I'm that guy. I'm that husband.

I'm also that guy who hasn't had a "real" job in over ten years. I've been working at creating an online presence that is inspiring and practical for my followers and provides the family with some income. It's been a slow process, but my wife has been behind me from day one. I'm the luckiest guy on the planet.

So, if you're a husband who desperately wants to have a successful career, it takes a lot of time, effort, and money.

However, don't create your "empire" at the expense of your wife and kids. I succeeded at building a thriving ministry and almost lost my wife.

Here is what I did to keep her in my life.

And, this is what I'm doing now to build a balanced future.

INTRODUCTION

Whether you've been married for one week or thirty years, there are certain things you need to have or develop in your marriage to keep it fresh, new, and alive.

No doubt you have a few things on your list that you practice consistently to make your spouse feel loved, special, noticed, excited, secure, relaxed, safe, and ________________.

And I do not doubt that you already practice some of these practical suggestions with amazing results. That's fantastic.

My goal is to outline several actions a husband can take to make his wife feel like she did on the day he proposed to her, on her wedding day, and even on her wedding night. You want her to feel more loved today than ever before.

Do one of them. Do all of them. Do something. It is the idle husband or wife, the inactive participant, who has no clue how great they have it by being married to the one they love.

Remember, your spouse said, "I do" to you, and you said the same.

So, if your business is starting to take off but your marriage is on its last breath, let's do some CPR and revive it slowly and deliberately. No matter how low it may be, you owe it to yourself and to your wife to give it your best effort from this day forward. Don't wait for her to start anything. You need to be the one to breathe new life into your lives together. Don't give up.

If your business is struggling, but your marriage is fully alive and thriving, let's find a way to kick-start your business without losing your wife in the process. No matter how great either one is, you know it's because you worked at it together. So, why don't you surprise your loved one with something new, something unexpected? Build on what you already have.

Throughout this entire book, I want you to keep two critical words in mind:

Communicate and Give

Unless you're willing to communicate with your spouse, you're wasting your time. Your spouse may reject your attempts at first. Don't give up. Keep at it. Be honest, and don't get defensive. Develop good timing for heart-to-heart talks. It will take effort and practice. You'll figure it out.

I know you give a lot of time and effort to your business—online or otherwise. I know I do. Unless you're willing to give time and effort to your marriage, you can forget it. You have to be ready to give without being appreciated and serve without reciprocation. (Sounds like a business). Marriage is hard work, and someone has to pick up the shovel first and start digging. Pick up the shovel.

One more thing before we move on.

Define success in your business.

No one decides whether or not you are a success except you. Success is relative to your specific and unique business. There is no dollar amount associated with success unless you are the one putting on that distinctive label.

I do know this: The concept of "more" can be dangerous. Contentment keeps "more" from sucking up your time and keeping you blind to your own family.

Contentment is not meant to stifle growth. It is, however, intended to keep us grounded so we can focus our best efforts on what means the most—our mate and family. So grow your business, learn contentment, and keep your wife in clear focus.

This book resulted from being married, yet completely blurred to what being married means actually, and how it affects your business if you're not completely clear and in focus with your wife.

HOW TO LOSE YOUR WIFE
WITHOUT EVEN TRYING

Sometimes a loss is the best thing that can happen.
It teaches you what you should have done next time.
Snoop Dogg

The best way to guarantee a loss is to quit.
Morgan Freeman

We'd moved around a little too much for my liking, but when I was offered a youth ministry position in North Carolina, I knew we'd be staying there for a while. The prospect of settling down appealed both to me and my wife, Lisa.

We settled in, and I got to work.

The youth group started growing. The church was loving and accepting. We felt at home for the first time in several years.

Lisa decided on a career path.

When we got married, I was a college graduate, but she was just out of high school. Eighteen years old and willing to follow me and my "calling" wherever that might lead. I would never have done that when I was eighteen. Then again, the right motivation will get a person to do just about anything. I was her motivation and her salvation from another life.

Lisa considered becoming a math teacher. That idea quickly went away. It just didn't add up. She loved helping others, so she decided to pursue a career in nursing.

She enrolled at the local community college and dove in.

Eventually, my routine meant spending more and more time away from the house. Leadership within our denomination's district structure involved summer camps, mission trips, retreats—all stuff that demands time.

Lisa graduated as a Certified Nursing Assistant. Yay. I thought that was over. Nope. With a six-day break, she jumped right back in to pursue her full associate degree as a registered nurse. Yay, again.

With no children yet, she was doing her thing, and I was doing mine. Hers was developing a career. Mine was to overdo it.

Somewhere during our seventh year of marriage, Lisa decided she was a little homesick and wanted to take a vacation with mom and dad for a week. Sure. Why not? I was busy with all the stuff I was doing. I figured I'd have more time to do it for a week without a lot of distraction.

Yeah, my only thought was that my marriage was a distraction. I was an idiot.

Off she went to New Brunswick for a week. Off to work I went, saving the world, one kid at a time, one meeting at a time, one committee at a time.

Then came the phone call.

Lisa called from her parents' home and told me she was going to see an old friend from high school. It was her former boyfriend. I said, "Sure. Why not?" I was oblivious to any thought of her leaving me. It never crossed my mind.

Then, there was the second phone call.

"I don't think I want to come back."

Wait? Did I hear that right? She just said she wasn't coming back. Not coming back to me? Why?

Why not? Exactly. We had no child to worry about, only the dog. Lisa never bonded with the dog. Just me, and I was hardly ever there. I was too busy trying to be successful in my chosen profession. So, what was she giving up?

She started giving up on me. She married me, but I wasn't there for her. I was quite clueless about what being a great husband should be, even after seven years of practice. (Practicing all the wrong things doesn't work very well, but we'll get to that later.) I became that guy who was doing his best to be a successful failure and succeeding. When you think about it, my wife wasn't giving up much.

Wait a minute.

She didn't say she was leaving me. She said she was "thinking about" leaving me. She said she was "thinking about" not coming back. She hadn't entirely made up her mind yet. I still had a shot.

Commence begging over the phone.

"Lisa, don't leave me. My career will be ruined."

Yup, that was the first thing I thought of. Who was going to hire a divorced youth pastor in the '80s in the conservative Bible belt? No one.

That wasn't my best argument. It was very poor begging on my part.

I took another shot at it.

"Lisa, I don't know what I've done, but I'll do whatever it takes to keep you as my wife. I'll do anything. Just come home to me and give me one more chance."

It was true. I was still clueless about what I'd done wrong completely in the dark. First things first. Get her home, then figure it out.

After more groveling and crying (I'm a very emotional guy, so I'm the one crying here—lots of crying), she said she'd come back, and we'd talk.

Please bear in mind that I was serious about doing whatever I had to do to keep her—literally anything. It sounds like a line any guy would use to halt a situation and get a second shot. And it is. But I was serious about it.

Between the time we hung up, and the time I picked her up at the airport, I made up my mind to quit my job, change careers, whatever. I would do anything to keep her in my life. I was convinced that a divorce would be devastating, that I would never love again, never find intimacy again, never have a church ministry again, never, in short, recover. I was convinced that my world would end the minute Lisa said she wasn't coming back. I was never going to let that happen. It wasn't going to happen to me. It wasn't going to happen to my wife.

I had to be serious about this. A sudden and enormous shift in my priorities had to take place. If I weren't serious, I would be divorced.

Lisa came home. We talked. She talked, and I learned to listen. I learned to open my eyes and ears to understand what she needed from me as a husband.

Lisa told me she was going to see her old boyfriend, and that hadn't bothered me at all. It wasn't until years later that she told me what had happened that night. Lisa cried in his arms, and he made her an offer. He said that if she left me, he'd take care of her, marry her, and they would have a life together. He assured her that she would have a soft landing and a safe future.

He made it easy for her to say no to me. Fortunately for both of us, Lisa hadn't been willing to give up on our marriage yet. It only takes one more chance to turn things around, as long as both parties in a marriage learn to turn together.

The rest of that year is still fuzzy to me. I know we talked more than we ever had before. I learned to say no to more meetings and ministerial stuff. I spent more time with Lisa, and she spent more time with me.

Over time, we figured it out. Together.

That was our seventh year of marriage. The dreaded "7-Year-Itch" had almost done us in. Instead, we said YES to year number eight.

It's now been 35 years, and our situation changed dramatically. What? You think I'd still be a youth pastor? It didn't work out that way. God led us in new directions.

Lisa is a family nurse practitioner heading up her clinic. Four 10-hour workdays. She also works Fridays at the university clinic to keep her hand in that area of care. On top of that, she has a part-time gig at an Urgent Care Facility and another one at the behavioral health unit down in Denver. Hilariously, she's thrilled doing all of it.

Me? I make sure she can do all of that. I am her biggest cheerleader and support. After all, I'm her husband. I work from home as a writer and a blogger.

By design, my time is flexible. I get my stuff done, but I take care of whatever else needs to be taken care of so my wife can do what she loves to do.

We've found a way to make our lives work together. That's what every marriage does. You find a way. Trial and error is part of the process, but you keep at it together.

What follows are seven areas Lisa and I focus on to make our marriage work. Because we work hard in these areas, I have the time to build my business online.

She works hard for many long hours every week. Getting a new business up and running also takes a lot of time and effort. Entrepreneurs tend to go after their dreams full speed ahead. Don't leave your wife in your wake as you do so. Focusing on your marriage and family first gives you the support and time to go after your dreams.

Let these points come into focus in your marriage, and they'll work to keep it healthy. I'm convinced that it will give your business a boost of success as well.

EMBRACE UNWAVERING OWNERSHIP

*When you make a commitment to a relationship,
you invest your attention and energy in it more
profoundly because you now experience
ownership of that relationship.*
Barbara de Angelis

I take ownership of every mistake I've ever made.
Paul Runyon

*We were together, but we weren't,
you know, together.*
Bill McConnell

Secret #1:
The best way to lead is by sacrifice.

Leadership is not a dictatorship.

When we lived in North Carolina, a lovely young lady in our church began dating a nice young man. Seems logical enough. Over time they fell in love. She started attending his church some, and he, in turn, visited her home church. Eventually, they attended his church more.

No big deal.

He asked for her hand in marriage; she accepted. Congratulations!

As their wedding day approached, they planned the wedding and wrote their vows. He insisted she state in her vows that she would "submit wholly to his authority."

As I understand it, the young couple had many long discussions about this language. The more the young lady expressed her reluctance to use those words in her vows, the more contentious he became, even bordering on verbal abuse. It wasn't long before she broke off the engagement. His insistence that she promise to "submit" scared her. She saw a side of him that had nothing to do with leadership or love. It was a trait she felt would be dangerous to her over the long term.

This young woman had the wisdom to get out before experiencing more of that side of him firsthand.

"Wives, submit yourselves to your own husbands," is found in Ephesians 5:22. It appears this young man was stuck on this phrase. It isn't even the whole verse. Furthermore, he missed the context of the entire passage.

There's so much more to marriage than having a wife "submit."

The whole verse reads, "Wives, submit yourselves to your own husbands as you do to the Lord." The wife is to submit to her husband in the same way she submits to Christ.

And here are the next two verses

For the husband is the head of the wife as Christ is the head of the church, his body, of which he is the Savior. Now as the church submits to Christ, so also the wives should submit to their husbands in everything. Ephesians 5:23-24 NIV

Well, this sounds pretty one-sided doesn't it? Not really. Don't forget the role of Christ in this paragraph. He is the key to it all.

Christ never wielded His leadership over His disciples as a taskmaster. He never sat them down and ordered them to submit to His leadership.

They followed Him because they believed Him. They believed He was who He said He was. They believed it because He lived it. They believed it because He could back it up.

He said to them, as He does to all of us, "Follow me." He never said, "Follow me, or else."

He never said, "Submit to me, or else." There is no love in such a statement.

Christ never beat down His disciples. He loved them. He gave them a reason to follow Him. He gave them a reason to submit to Him.

He loved them as He loves us.

I guess the young groom-to-be decided not to see the verse in context, specifically the verse just before this passage. It introduces the very essence of this section.

Submit to one another out of reverence for Christ. Ephesians 5:21 NIV

In other words, if she has something to say, he needs to shut up and listen. If she has a better way of doing things, he needs to see the value of that and support her by doing it her way.

Marriage is an agreement between two people who have made vows to each other for life. It is not one person lording it over the other one.

Wait a minute. So, what about "Wives, submit yourself to your own husband"?

It's still there, but every marriage has two sides. What does this specific passage say about the husband's role?

Husbands, love your wives, just as Christ loved the church and gave himself up for her to make her holy, cleansing her by the washing with water through the word, and to present her to himself as a radiant church, without stain or wrinkle or any other blemish, but holy and blameless. In this same way, husbands ought to love their wives as their own bodies. He who loves his wife loves himself. After all, no one ever hated their own body, but they feed and care for their body, just as Christ does the church—for we are members of his body. Ephesians 5:25-30

That's a tall order for husbands to live up to! There's a lot more weight and responsibility put on the husband to love his wife than for the wife to submit to the husband.

It's a whole lot easier to submit than to love. Without spending much thought, you work every day submitting to the rules and guidelines set forth by your employer or company. You do it their way, or you don't work there anymore.

You submit every day to the laws of the road. Red means stop. Green means go. Yellow means speed up to get through the intersection. (Kidding) You don't think about it because it impacts you and your safety. However, you must decide whether or not you are going to stop or go at any given time regardless of the color of the light.

Christ submitted Himself to death on a cross for you, me, and the church. He loves us that much. Remember, Christ didn't *have* to go to the cross. He *chose* to go to the cross. He didn't *have* to submit. He *chose* to submit. He didn't *have* to suffer. He *chose* to suffer. He didn't have to do any of this, but He did. Why? He did it because He loves us.

So, if the husband fulfills his part of the agreement by loving his wife as honestly and intentionally as Christ loves the Church, his wife will have no problem submitting to him and respecting him. She will go with him to the ends of the earth because he is worth following. He will be worth submitting to and loving.

You are to own the responsibility for your marital bliss.

Suddenly, it sounds like the husband is responsible for making the marriage work. I wouldn't dump it on him altogether. But if the marriage is going to get better, may I strongly suggest that it starts with the husband?

Why the husband? Let me explain to you the key roles of the husband in the marriage.

He is to lead by example

Be the man a woman would want to follow. There's only one way to do that: Love her like no other, but love God first. Fall in love with Christ and your wife will fall in love with you all over again. But keep this in mind: being the example has nothing to do with speaking, talking, preaching, or teaching. Adhere to the teaching attributed to St. Francis of Assisi, "Preach the Gospel at all times, and, when necessary, use words."

If you live it first, it is more believable for her to hear when the time comes.

He is to lead from behind

- Be the husband who wants his wife to succeed in whatever she desires.

- Be the guy who gently pushes when she doubts her abilities, but you know she can do it.

- Be the one to catch her when she falls.

- Be the one to help her turn around and head in the right direction.

- Be the one she knows is always there but is never in her face.

Be that guy for *her*.

He is to lead from the side

Be the husband who's right there with her:

- Ready to catch her when she falls.

- Ready to hold her hand and tell her she can do it.

- Ready to whisper in her ear how marvelous, beautiful, and capable she is.

- Ready to hug her and congratulate her when she succeeds.

- Ready to kiss her cheek and remind her that you love her no matter what.

- Ready to face everything together.

He is to lead from his knees.

Guys, does your wife know you pray for her every day? Do you pray for her every day? Do you pray with her every day?

Here's a secret just for husbands. Women love godly men—real, holy men—not men who go to church and blend in. They love men who sincerely pray. They love men who are hungry for God. They do.

Why do women love godly men?

Because when God comes first in his life, his lady, his wife, knows she's in good hands. She knows he will have her best interests at heart. She knows he will treat her like no other. She knows she's safe, secure, and loved.

And when she knows this, she has no problem submitting to him, because he will love her as Christ loves His church.

He is to lead with a plan

In a healthy marriage, the husband and wife move in the same direction together.

When Lisa married me, I had a plan. She married into that plan. She rolled with the highs and lows of my career and began to forge her own. Whatever we did in life, we decided together or at least agreed together to go in that direction.

At the same time my career began to shift and change, her career began to grow and blossom. Had I not been behind her in her efforts, we would have been scrambling to keep our family together financially. We learned to work together toward our dreams.

Husbands, I tell you this from experience. Support your wife in reaching her dreams. You have no idea how this will pay off someday down the road.

It doesn't matter whose plan it is or if the plan changes. Lead confidently toward fulfilling that plan. Support each other and head in the same direction together. It is incredible how different careers can complement each other. Keep that in mind when career curveballs get thrown your way.

As you read through the rest of this book, I pray you will understand the responsibility both a husband and a wife to make your marriage amazing.

Husbands: It is the coward who believes his wife isn't worth it. You're wrong. She is worth it. As a man, you asked her to marry you, didn't you? You said, "I do," didn't you? It was worth it back then, and it's worth it now.

Wives: You said "yes" to his proposal. (Maybe you asked him. That's cool.) He said, "I do," right back to you. You saw that he was worth it.

Well, it's time for both of you to prove to each other that it was worth it.

To both of you: You are the coward if you say the other must change before you will. You're passing off the responsibility as too much work. You want your spouse to take the first step. Why? Why are you waiting for that? Your love may be thinking, "If he will just make a little effort, I know things will get better."

How many marriages ended because both parties were waiting for the other to do something first?

I saw a billboard advertising a divorce lawyer. It said, "Life's short. Get a divorce." It's the coward who says he wants to start over. In my opinion, too many people who want to start over. Who's to say it won't happen again? You can't keep starting over. The expense alone will likely kill both of you.

Being together as God intended lays the foundation for business excellence.

Gordon MacDonald, in his book, *Ordering Your Private World*, says, "Driven people get things done, but they may destroy people in the process."

Entrepreneurs are driven people. You want to get this business going. You want to be successful, and you want to do it for your family. Think "Walter White" without the illegal making and dealing of meth. However, if you do it at the expense of, or even in spite of, your wife and family, the price is too high.

Family first, then business. This is the only way it works if you want to have both.

Guys, "Man up!"

Take matters into your own hands. Take responsibility. Be the guy whose wife's friends say, "I wish I had a husband like yours."

Yes, this happened to me. What a positive ego boost it was, too. I was careful not to let it go to my head. If I did, I would no longer be that guy. I like being that guy. My wife loves it too.

So take the responsibility. Step up to the plate. Be the one who wants the ball at the end of the game when it's all on the line. Add more sports analogies like these right here. I know there's some more out there.

Take the first step in making your marriage more amazing than it is already.

Ladies, "Step up."

Take matters into your own hands. Take responsibility. Be the lady who makes your husband's friends jealous, and not just because of how attractive you are. Beautiful women are everywhere, but very few are like you—amazing and worth the effort of loving for a lifetime.

Be the woman in his life who isn't nagging all the time. Be the woman who helps in every area of the marriage. Be the woman responsible for making him the man that he is and can be. Be that woman for him, and your marriage will be amazing.

Now, let's get practical.

HANDCRAFT MEMORABLE MORNINGS

I wake up some mornings and sit and have my coffee and look out at my beautiful garden, and I go, 'Remember how good this is because you can lose it.
Jim Carrey

I'm horrible in the mornings. I'm grumpy.
Hugh Grant

Secret #2:
A good morning will make her day.

Back then.

I was leaving for early morning prayer meetings and catching up with kids before school. I thought she just wanted to get up when it was convenient for her. In my mind, I was doing her a favor. I thought I was giving her time to herself.

Sometimes I never told her I was going. I just assumed she knew my schedule. An assumption is never a good thing, especially in a marriage.

What I was doing was leaving her alone. She was alone for those mornings. She got up alone and couldn't find me anywhere. She couldn't even call me. It was the '80s—back in the day before cell phones.

So, I said "no" to some of those "ministry opportunities" and took care of her. I didn't do it every day, but I did do it more and more. The times when I would leave early, we talked about it the night before. I never wanted her to feel alone again.

One morning, my wife was in a terrible mood. She didn't sleep well, waking up three or four times during the night with hot flashes. She had to get up at 5:15 a.m. She felt rushed, even though she wasn't. Knowing that Lisa was leaving, our dog wouldn't leave her alone—nudging, pawing, circling—the way she behaves every morning.

By the way, our dog, Ziggi, is a purebred Australian Shepherd. She has energy all day long, beginning first thing in the morning.

We usually pray together before Lisa leaves, but on this day she even felt rushed with this effort. It just wasn't her morning. She dragged her tired body out the door and off to work, which she does at this time four days a week.

It doesn't always go like this, but this morning was pretty rough for her.

How can you, as a husband make your wife's morning as smooth and worry-free as possible? How can you make her worst morning as transition-free and as smooth as it could be? Try doing as much as possible so that she has to do as little as possible. Don't overwhelm yourself. Doing just one little thing for her will mean a lot.

When considering the following recommendations, bear in mind that my wife leaves before me on these early week-day mornings. If this isn't your situation, don't worry. It's all easily adaptable. Here's what I do for my wife.

I always get up before she does. Always.

Her time may be limited in the morning, but mine is more open-ended. Just because I don't have to rush off early doesn't give me license to sleep in. I get up, and I get dressed. I'm serious. I don't want her to leave with the impression that I sleep while she has to go to work earlier. That could be an open door for possible resentment down the road.

This past week I had to finish up some work specific to getting this book finished on schedule. I told Lisa I had to stay up late, and I did. I got to bed after midnight, yet I was up before her at 5:20 a.m. It wasn't easy, but I did it for her.

I plug in her hair straightener.

Wow, that took two to three seconds at most. Whew, glad I got that done. It means Lisa walks in and does her hair without waiting for the thing to heat up. It's the little things that make the difference in saving time and easing her routine. She remembers the little things, and thanks me for them.

The coffee is ready the night before. I push the button.

We just bought a brand new Breville YouBrew, pricey, but a whole lot better than the last coffeemaker we had. Yes, it has an automatic timer I could use, and I do on occasion. Or, I push the button. It was prepped the night before, so, I made coffee for both of us. It reinforces the idea that I'm up as well, even though all I did was make coffee.

Next, I'm not going to crash for three hours as soon as she leaves the house. I could, and sometimes I want to, but I don't.

Why? Because if she asks me what I did after she left, I won't lie to her. I tell her the truth. She would become envious of that extra sleep. Over time, this won't sit well with her. So, I stay up. It's better for me anyway.

At this point, it's safe to say I am a morning person. My wife is not—all the more reason to give her attention first thing in the morning.

If she needs something quickly, I get it for her.

I'm not doing anything else, so I try to be ready to help with whatever little things might ease her routine. As I said, it's the little things she'll remember as special. If you're both getting ready at the same time, think of one thing you can get for her. You know her routine, so offer to help. It won't throw you off if you plan to do it.

Her breakfast and lunch are ready and waiting for her.

It's done the night before and in the fridge. (Yes, I get it ready for her. I'm that kind of guy.) Breakfast is yogurt she takes with her. Often, lunch is what we had for dinner the night before. I make extra for this purpose. Coffee is ready. There's an apple for a snack. All she has to do is not forget to take it with her. That's my job as well. Figure out her lunch schedule, if she doesn't already have one, and own that responsibility.

I pour her coffee in the travel mug and know exactly how to fix it for her.

I always tease about how she likes a little coffee with her Splenda and creamer. Does your wife know exactly how to fix your coffee for you? It doesn't matter whether she does or not, because you're preparing hers, not the other way around. It takes less than a minute—no sweat.

If you haven't figured it out by now, I'm a bit of a coffee snob. I make no apology for this. So is our daughter. She won't apologize either. Lisa, not so much. Now, however, my wife expects coffee perfection from me. I don't know why she cares, because she likes her coffee additives more than the coffee itself. I'm sure there's a need for caffeine as well but let's not get into that now.

I walk her to the car, even though it is just in the garage.

Briefcase, lunch bag, coffee travel mug, whatever else she has to lug, I help her get it there which makes her feel valued. Doing this shows her I care about her. It tells her that I value her work routine. It shows her I am attentive to her situation. It means something to her because I care about what she's doing every day for the sake of the family.

We pray together before she leaves.

Not a long prayer, just a blessing for her day which takes under a minute. I hug my wife. Finally, we've trained the dog to leave us alone so we can do this uninterrupted and without getting taken out at the knees by her insistence that we toss the ball immediately. You can do the same thing.

I kiss her goodbye.

Doing this tells her I love her. It leaves the impression that I did all of this in the morning because I love her. The more value I can add to her morning the better it is for her at the time and for us later on.

The key is planning.

If you plan the morning ahead of time, there is less stress for both of you. And the less pressure there is for your wife and you, the more amazing her morning will be, and she'll thank you for it.

Now, all of this could take place in less than half an hour. It takes less than that for us. It's not even 6:00 a.m. yet, and Lisa's off to work. I could go back to bed and sleep for another three hours. I don't, but it's an option. I could watch

SportsCenter for an hour or so, but I don't. You won't either. You have your daily responsibilities to tackle.

Because I have the time she doesn't, I make every effort to make her morning as smooth as possible. I make her mornings more bearable and manageable. She leaves knowing I've done some things for her benefit. Less stress equals a fantastic morning for her.

I've just described for you what I do for my wife every morning when she heads off to work.

My guess is you have one huge question you're just dying to spring on me. Here's what I think it is and here is my answer.

"Are you a trained (broken), submissive husband?"

Absolutely not. Are you kidding me? What an absurd thing to even suggest. My wife is busting her tail to make an income for the family. You're probably doing the same thing. Or you may be unemployed or in transition between the old job and the new one. (You know, unemployed.) Or maybe you're building an online empire that isn't making any income yet. How long have you been there?

What I am doing is supporting her efforts as she goes off to work. Good for me.

Now, let's apply this concept to your situation. As the loving husband that you are, what would make your wife's morning amazing?

Your wife doesn't work, but you do.

Great. You can still do some of these things.

- After you get coffee, make sure there's enough for two.

- Pray with your wife before you leave for work. If she's still in bed, sit down for a few seconds and pray together.

- If she is still asleep, sit or stand beside the bed and pray. If she is faking sleep (she'd never do that, right?), she'll know what you're doing and love you that much more for doing it.

- Kiss her good-bye. In bed? Kiss her goodbye. Still asleep? Kiss her goodbye.

- What's the first thing your wife needs when she gets up in the morning? Do a little prep and get it ready if possible.

- Leave a Post-It Note with a thought on it every morning. Okay, maybe not every morning but a few times a week at least. It'll take you less than a minute. If not every morning, one or two times a week. Keep your wife on her toes as to when or where it'll be. (The game's afoot.)

Your wife leaves for work after you; you're the one who has to get to work early.

See above. It's all possible with a little bit of planning. Even if you do just one thing new, something that your wife doesn't expect you to do, it is the first step toward creating a morning that's memorable for her.

The key is to do something new, unexpected, AND to continue to do it on a regular basis.

One idea is to be your wife's alarm clock. She could wake up to some pre-programmed sound on her phone, or YOU could be that personal touch every morning for her.

HINT: Don't forget to do it. Don't miss one single morning once you promise to get her up. I did once or twice, and she was late getting to work. Hey, it happens. Nobody's perfect. It was entirely my fault, but it raised her stress level for that entire day. Nobody needs to start his or her day like that. On the other hand, accidents do happen. Both of you will get over it.

What if both of you get up and leave at the same time?

If this is the case, both of you should know each other's routine very well. Right? So, figure out one thing your wife does that you can do instead. Then do it. Take ownership of that one thing.

Yes, it's one more thing for you to do, but it's one less thing for her to do. She will notice your effort to make her morning a little less stressful and appreciate you for it.

Oh, and always get up before your wife, even if it's just by a minute. Beat the other out of bed. It is important because you don't want to leave even a trace of an idea in her head that you got to stay in bed longer.

Getting up first is easy for me because I have to go to the bathroom. Fortunately, we have two bathrooms. If there were only one, my wife would get to use it first. Guys, don't make her wait for you for even a second. A woman and her bathroom in the morning are nothing to mess with. I know the dangers of this firsthand. You don't want to go there.

Get this into your head.

The more supportive you are of your wife first thing in the morning, the less stress she will have.

Also, she has less stress during her day whether she's at home or at her job. This is a good thing for you, her, and the family.

Being together with your morning rituals sets the stage for a more productive day.

Your wife heads off to work feeling she's been taken care of. Wives love that feeling. When you start your day with her in mind, you know she is your number one priority. More importantly, she knows it. When she leaves, your mind is free to do what you do. You're taking care of business by taking care of her first.

Now, if your wife doesn't work and you work from home, I see the following take place. You get up early and get to work. Writing, creating, developing, whatever it is you're doing. She knows your routine, and you know hers. When she gets up, that is your cue to take a break and give her your attention—breakfast, a walk together, time together. It doesn't have to take all morning. It shouldn't. When you stop what you're doing to give her attention, she knows and feels how important she is to you. As much as possible, fashion your morning around her schedule. She will see your efforts and know you need time for work. She will be flexible with your schedule when she knows how flexible you are with yours for her benefit.

An Idea

Prerecord a personal message on your wife's phone and set it as her wake-up alarm preference. Surprise her with your sexy voice and gentle message to get her out of bed.

CREATE REMARKABLE EVENINGS

*My wife and I have a tradition of popcorn and videos
with our kids on Friday evenings.*
Oswald Boateng

*I know I've got a degree. Why does that mean I have to
spend my life with intellectuals? I've got a lifesaving cer-
tificate, but I don't spend my evenings diving for a rubber
brick with my pajamas on.*
Victoria Wood

Secret #3:
A little effort will go a long way.

Being on staff in a new church in a new city, I wanted to
impress my boss as anyone would. Most church meetings
happen in the evenings. Sunday night church (Yeah, it was
the '80s) Midweek youth group, discipleship groups, leadership groups, monthly board meetings, district planning
meetings, and so on.

"Oh, Bill would be great on this planning committee. It
is his area of expertise."

It was great to be wanted and needed in this new job, but
it sucked for our marriage. Somehow, I equated job success
with marriage success.

"I'm proud of my husband for doing so well."

She may have said that early on, but it got old quickly for her.

I learned to say "No" to some of these things as well. Date night became a non-negotiable ritual for us. I refused to let the business get in the way of our marriage as it had in the past.

Some would argue the following:

- I'm doing this for the family.

- I'm working hard for the family.

- I'm creating a new business from home, so I can have more time for the family.

All of this is great, but don't do any of it at the expense of the family.

I'm sorry, but I can't help but think about the TV series *Breaking Bad* and Walter White right now.

"Everything I've done, I've done for my family."

Walter White said that for five seasons while slowly tearing his family to shreds. In the final episode, he finally admitted that he did it for himself. He was good at it, he said. It made him feel alive. (If you don't have a clue what this is in reference to, you'll just have to watch the series.)

That was my attitude. Our youth group grew from 15 to 115 in one year. I was "Super Youth Pastor Guy." There should have been a T-shirt or cape or something. I traded in that imaginary cape for another one, a better one. I wanted a new identity. "Super Husband" sounded much better—better status and less wording. You know, for the T-shirt.

My evenings became our evenings for the first time in our marriage. Lisa started to see that she was my first priority instead of my job. Never sacrifice a successful marriage because you're gone four nights a week.

Let's skip ahead to today.

As I explained earlier, Lisa works 10+ hours a day, 4 days a week at her primary job, and does other part-time and volunteer work as well. (She redefines the Type A personality. I can barely keep up.) She works hard. When she comes home, she needs a break.

Because I know this, and since I work from home, there are a few things I want her to have when she gets home.

Again, this is what I do for my wife in our present circumstances. Any or all of this can be recreated or adjusted to fit your situation. Just be creative.

I want her to relax

If she's not relaxed, I won't be either. Since I schedule my own time, I'm flexible in what I can do for her. So, when she comes home, I want her to feel welcomed and appreciated for the hard work she puts in on behalf of the entire family.

I want her to feel that her efforts are appreciated

Since she's bringing in a much steadier income than I am, I want to show her appreciation.

Here are some things that I do.

Supper is ready

This is a well-planned effort on my part, so it takes less time than scrambling for supper ideas an hour before Lisa arrives. Planning alleviates my stress as well as hers. So, get on a schedule. I used to make a huge pot of spaghetti sauce or my famous chili. Either one of these will last us two to three days. It also got us a little fatter than we needed to be. Now I have better supper options in my cooking repertoire that are healthy for both of us. You should try my healthy, diet-friendly chicken fajitas.

If possible, I meet her at the door

The dog usually beats me down the stairs. I take my cues from the dog, only without the barking. Lisa has the same stuff to lug back in that she took out in the morning. Since I helped her get it out, I help her get it back in which helps me to check her mood. Sometimes she's good; sometimes she's super tired. If I can gauge her mood, I can treat her accordingly. Yes, you need to be that attentive. It may not be that big of a deal to you, but it is a big deal to her.

Figure out the timing

Having supper ready when she gets home is sometimes a challenge. She gets home anywhere from 5:45 p.m. to 7:00 p.m. depending on how her day goes. So I give it my best shot. She sees the effort, and that's what's important. Your situation may be more exact. I'm happy for you.

Order is evident

If she comes home to crap laying everywhere from a project I've been working on all day, she will probably not be very happy.

I don't know if all women are like this, but my wife knows how she left things. If I put one thing away before she gets home, she notices and is happy. If your family is the amazingly clean, put-it-all-away-all-the-time type, that's great. That's not our family, so she notices any effort to clean up a little. When your wife sees you've made an effort, that's a good thing.

Clean up after supper

Why wouldn't you? In theory, it only takes ten minutes to tidy up the kitchen and put the dishes in the dishwasher. It should be no big deal. She notices the effort you put into it and appreciates you for it. Or, if she's used to doing it, pitch in and help her.

Let her know your evening schedule

You may have something planned. The last thing your wife needs is to be surprised that you and the guys are modifying the Jeep in the garage for the next four hours. Knowing your schedule in advance eases her stress. So, communicate what's going on.

Give her the space she needs

Your wife may need uninterrupted, alone time to chill and unwind. Her space may include you. She may need you to give her some attention. My wife likes to read her Kindle. Sometimes she needs interaction and conversation. I'm there for her. There are times when she needs to exercise, and we prefer to do that together. We used to run. Lately I've discovered that running causes an aching back. So, there are times when we go to the park where I sit in the car while she runs. I take something I need to do (read, iPad, whatever) while she does a few laps. Figure out your wife's need for space and accommodate that need.

Remember

- You spent the day apart from each other. You have no idea what she may have gone through in her job.

- You spent the day doing whatever you do, with its stress level and pressures. Your wife may need to know you need some space.

- You spent the day thinking up ways to ease your wife's stress when she gets home. That alone may raise your stress level.

- Hopefully, you just spent the day pursuing your passion and so did your spouse. If her job, or yours, isn't your passion, both of you need to reassess how you spend your days. Just sayin'.

Find a way to give your wife the time and attention she needs when she gets home.

Being together in your evening rituals means you've learned to transition from work to wife.

When you leave your work for the day, then leave your work for the day. Giving your wife time every evening screams that your time with her has priority. There are times when my wife tells me to turn off the computer and spend time with her. As hard as it is sometimes, my goal is never to have her say that to me.

I know how it can get. You get this great idea and you want to record it somewhere so you don't forget. It may be an article, a product, or a topic to explore and develop for future use. This happens to me all the time. I get the idea down on my phone or tablet, but I've learned to leave it there. It only takes a minute to do this. Capture it quickly and forget it until the next morning. Have a system where you record ideas in one spot, app, or note, that you come back to review and refine.

It is the "notebook on the nightstand" idea. Don't lose the idea. Don't sacrifice any sleep. In this case, don't lose your focus on your wife or what you're doing for her.

Ideas come into my mind quickly and leave at the same speed. Capturing them is critical. I'm sure I've lost a few ideas because of that speed chase and not bothering to record them because my focus is on my wife. I'm okay with that. You should be as well.

Again, the primary goal is to make this time as stress-free as possible for your wife. The less stress there is, the better it will be for all involved. It is a win/win situation. You ease her stress, and she understands you're doing all of this for her benefit. If she relaxes, feels cared for, and secure, even though she's the one who may be working while you're getting your platform built, you reap the benefits of your efforts to make her feel special in the evening.

Now, at this point, you may be thinking, "This won't work for me. Our schedules are completely different. This'll never work. You're an idiot. Good luck. I'm outa here."

I get that, but I'm not an idiot. Look at the bigger picture. The goal is not to do what I do; it is to make your spouse's evenings more memorable. Your goal is to own the evening by making them amazing for the one you love. Over-the-top extravagance is not the goal here. Trying to top your last great effort will eventually lead to big letdowns for both of you.

Remember, the term "amazing" is relative. I grew into what I now do for my wife. It took several years of adding things, many little things, which I now do to make her evening a little less stressful.

So doing just one new thing regularly to help your wife out may make her evening little a more amazing.

NOTE: Don't make a big deal out of this. Try to do it matter-of-factly. If it appears you're doing all this to get something, "amazing" just left for the evening.

ESTABLISH HOUSEHOLD ROYALTY

In the past, people were born royal.
Nowadays, royalty comes from what you do.
Gianni Versace

Your part can be the king, but unless people are treating you like royalty, you ain't no king, man.
Jeff Bridges

Secret #4:
The royal treatment goes both ways (but it starts with the king).

As I struggled to patch up my marriage, I began to notice how I viewed and treated my wife. It wasn't good.

She was not my queen. She was more like Cinderella. There was royalty in there somewhere waiting to come out, but I kept her on a lower level without even realizing it. She may have been my queen, but I treated her like a person of low stature. Equality in our marriage was missing.

A huge reason I didn't treat her like my queen was that I didn't see myself as a king. So, I began holding the door for her. I held her hand every chance I had. I helped her on with her coat. I walked beside her instead of steaming on ahead like I always did, expecting her to keep up. Yes, I was that kind of guy, and it's a wonder she stayed with me as long as she did.

I discovered the more I treated her like a queen, the more she treated me like her king. A little attention and affection go a long way in the realm. My love for her became more tangible than ever, and she liked the attention. She deserved the attention. Our marriage was finally getting back on track. Due to my noble efforts, she saw hope in our future together.

I love a good TV series. As you already know, I am a die-hard fan of *Breaking Bad*. (This is my third reference already.) Walter White would do anything to take care of his family and guarantee their safety and happiness after he died. At least that's what he wanted everyone to believe.

(Warning: If you haven't seen the series, this will be a bit of a spoiler for you.)

It started that way; it didn't end up that way. Walt began with a goal to make enough money to take care of his family after he died. He had lung cancer.

It soon turned into Walter being in the "empire business." Eventually, it wasn't about the family anymore. It was all about him. His success. His empire.

When that happened, it tore the family apart. The damage was done. Finally, he told Skyler, his wife, that he didn't do it for them. He did it for himself. He was good at it.

Eventually, he accomplished his original purpose (taking care of the family financially), but at the expense and happiness of everyone involved.

His "reign" as king was at the expense of his queen. The price was too high. He died alone. His wife left alone. Forget the money. Lives deeply scarred forever.

Why? Because one person decided he was better than anyone else. No matter how hard he tried to "do it for the family," he was feeding his ego. It took his inevitable demise to get him to refocus on his original goal: making sure his family was cared for after his death.

When the *Breaking Bad* series ended, I eagerly looked for a replacement. I tried watching the series *Game of Thrones*. I lasted only six episodes. The subject matter and general content alone weren't to my liking.

My understanding of the series is that any main character in the series gets killed off and another main character rises. In any case, everyone was fighting for supremacy, the upper hand. Trust no one. Manipulate everyone. (Correct me if I'm wrong. As I stated, I only watched six episodes.)

This plot line makes for good TV entertainment for some, but in real life, the upper hand is never something a family member should desire.

Let me explain my concept of household royalty. It has nothing to do with power and authority. It has everything to do with how one person treats the person they love.

Understand this clearly; my wife is a queen. MY queen. I gave her this title. I can do that because of one simple fact. I'm the king. I like being the king. Wouldn't you?

This concept is all a matter of perspective, your Highness. Regardless of conflicting schedules, the guy, the husband, is the king of the family domain so to speak. No one needs to recognize this title except the husband and the queen, of course, and possibly the little princes and princesses. Maybe the dog. Cats are hopeless.

And because the two of you are together on this journey, there is no room for individual egos and selfish pursuits. You should not rule with an iron fist as many kings do. Queens, as well, should not take on the ruthlessness of being too controlling and impossible to please.

I'm not talking about Disney's vast and varied portrayals of royalty. In a marriage, there are real dangers to the idea of royalty going to your head or hers.

There is a real danger with the idea of being kings and queens together in a marriage. I've listed a few here—first the queens.

- Some queen want to sit permanently on the bigger throne at the expense of the king.

- Some queens feel they should get everything and anything they want at the expense of the income and budget.

- Some queens see themselves above the masses because of whom they're married to. It may be somewhat flattering to you as the king, but it is at the expense of benevolence and kindness.

- Some queens expect royal treatment that is above and beyond what any king would put up with.

- Some queens find themselves alone in their endeavors because few people can put up with them over time.

- Some queens think that they own the world, and the world is to do their bidding. If their king is "the world" to them, then he is in for a bad ride.

That may have been a little rough but, sadly, some queens are like that.

And now, kind sir, good king that you are, what follows is what you do not need to be in ruling from on high.

- Some kings look down on their queens because their "head of the royal household" status has gone to their heads.

- Some kings treat the rest of the family as beneath them in every aspect which makes the king an official idiot, a court jester.

- Some kings are created first in their minds. It is this royal perception they live outwardly. Ego can kill a marriage, leaving a king alone to rule nothing.

- Some kings expect to be treated as a superior leader even when they are not. They expect to be served by their families who they see as subordinates. They need to reread the second chapter. Seriously.

- Some kings don't have queens as mates. They see their spouse as a servant and a sole concubine. Yikes!

- And the big one—some kings keep their wives separated from family decisions because, he, the king, knows better. The queen is to follow along and do what she's told.

Can you think of any person who personifies these traits? I can. Dare I say it here? Several celebrities come to mind: egos and royal perception gone wild.

The attitude that "I'm better than you because ________" is a recipe for disaster in any marriage. Regardless of any worth or merit of the diva or the egotist, that attitude will kill a marriage.

Both of you are in it together. Work at it together.

Here's what NOT to do. Do NOT take on the attitude of an arrogant king toward your queen. Such a designation is degrading to both of you. Remember, it is all a matter of attitude.

- Lose your self-righteousness. Your grandiose sense of self helps no one and gains no friends. You cannot be much of a friend to your queen. She won't have it.

- On the other hand, do not place your wife so high on a pedestal that she won't be able to live up to the hype. Sadly, too many wives try to live up to their husband's expectations which may lead to a king taking advantage of her perceived position. Both of you will end up disappointed.

- A loving, heart-to-heart talk will put everything in perspective for both of you when it comes to regal affairs within the kingdom you call a family.

Speaking from a personal perspective.

My wife is not an arrogant queen. (Thank God!) She doesn't see herself as someone above me just because our work schedules and career paths are different. She doesn't expect me to do all of these things I'm suggesting to you. Yes, she'll miss them if I stop, but she doesn't take any of it for granted. We've had that discussion.

Now, my wife is not royalty, apart from being my queen. She's a hard working individual making the best of our chosen family situation. I work extremely hard to treat her like a queen without crossing the line to her becoming a diva. This treatment is my choice, not hers. If anything, she is my reluctant queen. Alternatively, I am her king, and that is her choice.

Why do I do all this "stuff" for her in the mornings, the evenings, and at other times during the day?

- I love her.

- I have a great deal of discretionary time, and she doesn't.

- I know what makes her feel special.

- I know what helps her out and what doesn't.

- I know how hard she works outside the home.

- I know she carries a lot of family responsibility.

- I know her efforts deserve recognition and she will get it nowhere else than from me.

With all of this in mind, here's my random list of things I do to treat her like my queen. I suggest you take this list and slowly incorporate them into your life with your queen, I mean, wife.

I do all of this for my wife, my queen because I love her. Think about it. What kind of king would act this way?

Pour her bath water

Yes, I do this every night for her. It's no big deal. It takes less than a minute to do. Clean the tub, add baby oil, and get a towel and washcloth ready. The only thing stopping a guy from doing this for his wife is attitude or the football game. Get over it. If you have to, wait for a timeout, then jump on it.

I even wash her back for her every time. It gives her some personal attention during every bath she takes. You can't go wrong doing this, and she will appreciate it.

Take care of the little things by thinking ahead and anticipating

Little things vary from person to person. The perceptive husband knows what he can do to make life a little easier for the one who needs that extra attention.

Since I do the shopping, I make sure I have the stuff she needs such as shampoo and conditioner. There are only two places in town that sell what she uses, so, I always buy two of each. (Why buy one when you can buy two for twice the price? Or maybe there's a sale. Either way.) I "hide" the extra one and wait. When she runs out, she'll ask me to get more—no problem when you have one hidden.

That reminds me, I have about a week to restock. I think I can fit that into my schedule.

Thinking ahead can surprise her. Often, I do wait for her to get a little upset when she runs out. Yes, I'm playing with fire, but I'm a husband who likes to live on the edge.

"Bill, did you get me shampoo today?"

"No, honey, I didn't."

"But I'm out. How will I do my hair?"

"Just check the bottle under the sink, dear."

"Hey, it's full."

"You're welcome."

As to the king in this home, the queen is happy.

Know what to leave alone

Since I do almost all the cleaning, there are some things and some places I refuse to go. Men, you will do well to know what these spaces are with your wife and steer clear.

Leave her clothes alone

I'll wash them and fold them, but I don't put them away. Why? A woman's closet is her domain, her organizational style, and her stuff. You cannot duplicate it. Don't even try. If you do, you will spend extra time finding her things for her because they aren't where she put them—this includes shoes. If you pick up her shoes and put them away, then also plan to find them for her when she needs them. Women have at least four times as many shoes as a guy. That's just a guess, and it may be low. Don't go there unless she asks.

Paperwork

The rule in our house is, "Don't open other people's mail, even if you know what it is." I leave hers alone. I stack it where she sees it every night, and if there's something I know needs quick attention, I let her know it's there. Then there's other paperwork that needs filing. She sees it first; then I put it away if she wants me to. It's best if only one person does the filing.

Her personal space

It may seem petty, but my wife's night table drives me crazy. It's her stuff, including all kinds of random "whatevers." I leave this area alone for one reason. It is recognition of her personal space. You need to recognize your spouse's specific areas of personal space and leave these alone, even if the disorganization drives you crazy. If you mess with it, it may mean increased stress for her and time she has to spend getting it back to the way she likes it. It's not worth it for you to go there. We share a home office. Her side is mostly crafts and a sewing machine. Mine is mostly business, home files, etc. We leave each other's area alone.

Projects

There is no way I'd go near my wife's projects. Anyone who knows their spouse knows that when they start a project, they're going to do it their way. I love to organize things; my wife not so much. I could make her life easier if she'd let me rearrange her stuff for her, but the key here is that it's hers. I'd go crazy if she reorganized my tools in the garage. It's the same for her.

Personal attention

I believe that women have a need to feel secure and loved. (Deep down, so do guys.) If you're the husband whose employment brings in irregular amounts monthly, like mine, she may feel a little less secure. Over time, I have learned what my wife needs to feel secure and loved. However, this varies from one person to another. I'm going to tell you what I do to make my wife feel she's getting the attention she needs. It may be different for your wife, so adapt and adjust these suggestions to meet your own needs.

Public displays of affection

Public displays of affection are unnatural for me. I'm not this kind of guy at all. My wife, however, loves it, so I make a point to hold her hand as much as possible. I hold the door for her and put my hand on the small of her back as she walks through it. I direct her a certain way by doing the same thing. I take the lead in this type of contact. She loves it.

Wise spending decisions

You don't need extra stuff. None of us do. Make financial decisions that honor the family budget. On one of our trips together I forgot to put my good pocketknife in the checked luggage, thus "volunteering" to give it to TSA. I felt I needed a suitable replacement, which was not an unreasonable request. My wife went with me to one of our favorite outdoor stores to pick out a new one. That Saturday, we walked out with a great new knife that cost $138.44. On Monday I came to my senses and took it back, obtaining a refund. I corrected a bad decision and let her know what I had done. (Seriously, who needs a $140 pocket knife?)

Making the wiser choice screamed volumes to her about my commitment to make better decisions regarding our finances.

Control your panic

Everyone panics. Some people handle it better than others. Having control instead of panicking may go totally against your personality. I believe it's perfectly okay to panic as long as you don't stay in that mode for very long. At some point, your wife needs to see you in control. Your calm demeanor will ease her anxiety.

Yes, I have been known to lose it, curl up in a fetal position in the corner, and cry, but I don't do it in front of her. She has enough to deal with without thinking her husband has lost it completely. Please don't say, "That's just not my personality." You may be the rock solid personality your wife loves. Not everybody is like that. Learning not to panic is a hard trait to master, a skill that develops over time. You can learn to hold it together when you need to. When you do, your wife will feed off your strength.

Please don't read too much into this and misunderstand. I'm not suggesting you walk around wearing the mask of staunch heroism all the time. You need to be honest and open with your wife, especially with your feelings. I've learned that when things start to come apart, my wife needs to be in charge. When the king gets over his breakdown, he provides leadership and hope once again. One of the most attractive traits a queen expects from her king is leadership with her, not in spite of her.

Don't let little decisions become an issue

There is no reason to go overboard on some things. Some people are adamant about making choices that aren't worth grumbling over. Don't be that guy. For example, when you go out to dinner together, make your time more enjoyable by not arguing over Asian cuisine or Tex-Mex. The bottom line is these decisions don't matter unless a particular type of cuisine might keep you in the bathroom for the rest of the night. Let your wife choose. She should know what upsets your tummy by now. It's no big deal. However, it may be for her. Letting her choose adds a little bit of value to her decision. She will notice your attention to her preference. Once you start doing this, she may very well return the gesture and let you pick. Good for you. Good for both of you.

Break up the routine

Plan a special meal at home to change things up. It's less expensive than going out. Randomly suggest going out for dessert afterward. The idea is to break up her routine. Also, doing something special continues to add to your persona as a husband who is attentive to the needs of his significant other.

Learn to be the flexible one

What if she is too tired to go out? It could happen if she's working a lot. I know you wanted Dairy Queen but get over it. Maybe going and getting it for the two of you would let her rest at home while you do the running. Being flexible shows her your attention to her needs, not yours—good job.

There's much more you can do to treat her like royalty. Get creative. Just don't let her think she's a queen with an attitude. Your efforts to make her feel special should never be misunderstood as the norm or expected.

Being together as household royalty means both are aware of the "business of the realm"

The business of the realm is what you do as king. You're creating a company. You're busting your butt to have a better life for yourself, your wife, and family. You are doing this for the family.

The 4-Hour Work Week, written by Tim Ferriss, was a ground-breaking NY Times bestselling book that drilled into our heads the idea that we can work less, make more, and have more time to do whatever we want. Countless numbers of people took him up on the offer. Many succeeded. Many failed.

I began following two different blogs about husbands and wives who left conventional job/home/vocation for something different. One husband convinced his wife to sell everything they had and hit the road. His idea was to travel around North America (and beyond) blogging, writing, pursuing photography, and so on. His focus was on minimal finances and maximum freedom.

This blogger was inspirational. To my knowledge, the family—yes, family with kids—are doing great. They had a financial plan and determined purpose. Both king and queen were on board. It worked.

The other blog, however, died after just a few months. They started with a great idea and feasible plan, but the king talked the queen into following along. Not only that, because her work was location-independent, he relied on her to bring in the cash while he tried to figure out his business along the way.

His last blog entry was the saddest I've ever read. He told his readers that his plans had failed, his wife left him, and he was, essentially, homeless. He shut down his dream and sunk back into traditional work once again.

It is very sad when the queen leaves the kingdom because she'd be happier as a commoner. Not only that, as a single commoner. While this has never happened to me, I feel it would be better to lose my wife to another man than to my inattentiveness and stupidity. I'm not willing to test this theory. Actually, I don't want to lose her for any reason.

Kings

I see myself as a king, and I make these little gestures of love from my situation and perspective. Most, if not all of these suggestions, are transferrable to your circumstances. See it from your castle. Think positively about it. DO NOT SAY, "That'll never work in my household." Or "You gotta be kidding me!"

I'm not kidding. It can work if you get a little creative. You may even shock your queen in ways you can't imagine. She may say something like, "Who is this knight-in-shining-armor and where has he been all these years?"

Do not correct her with the knight versus king status. Take the compliment and move on.

TACKLE THE LITTLE THINGS

It's the little details that are vital.
Little things make big things happen.
John Wooden

It has long been an axiom of mine that the little things are
infinitely the most important.
Arthur Conan Doyle

Secret #5:
A little time used wisely never goes unnoticed.

During that seventh year when I was patching up my marriage while continuing to do my job, we added to the stress by having a dog.

Now scientists and behaviorists agree that having a dog relieves stress and helps a family in countless ways. I wish that were the case during that year.

Our dog had epilepsy. It was quite severe. The added stress wasn't helpful to our delicate marital status. For the next two years, the dog only got worse. The drugs were expensive and ineffective—our inevitable decision to put the dog down made things worse.

During this time, I took on all the little things necessary to care for the dog. It was one less thing for Lisa to do, and one more thing for me to do. I did it anyway.

My care for our dog awakened a new revelation—although my wife is entirely healthy, I should give her the same care and attention. It was all about the details, the little things that I did for the dog to keep her functioning that made a difference for her. So, why can't I take care of the small things in our family, instead of expecting my wife to do it?

So, I started by doing the dishes. I thought Lisa was going to fall over. I was helping out around the house, and most of the jobs didn't require power tools.

This process has grown tremendously from that year to the present day.

There are dust bunnies everywhere! Our current dog is an Australian Shepherd named Ziggi. Not only that, she is an Aussie with a tail, a big bushy tail. Most Aussies have their tail docked at birth. Not so with ours. (She's European, I guess.) She adds so much to our lives—energy, excitement, companionship, fun, personality, hair everywhere, and so on. If you're a dog owner, you know what I mean about the dust bunnies.

It's just a fact: with dogs comes added work and maintenance. Their fur alone adds to the growth, size, and accumulation of dust bunnies. I hate dust bunnies.

I've heard that Aussies only shed two times a year, lasting six months each time. This statement is true.

Now, guess who deals with those bunnies and the dog? I do. Why? Because I'm the one who handles the majority of the household order and upkeep. Why would I do that? It's my choice because my time is more flexible than hers. (Both a blessing and a curse.)

Now, when you're busting your tail working from home—creating, writing, promoting, doing everything that it takes to get your independence up and running—that takes a lot of time. I know. I'm doing it as well. I'd work 24 hours a day for myself rather than 8 hours a day for anybody else. However, you cannot do that at the expense of household neglect.

Let me show you how to get a ton of housework done and take care of your business. I will tell you this right now. If you want to keep working from home, then working from home is not your priority. Your home is your priority. Keep that first, especially where your wife is involved, and she'll be extremely pleased with your choice to work at whatever you're doing.

Here are the details.

I am not maintenance-oriented. For me, it is a necessary evil. And since I'm the one who's home most of the time, I decided to put it all on my shoulders to get it done.

Now, since I hate it so much, I come at this challenge with two things in mind.

1. **I live by the Time/Effort Principle.** Everything I do at home to keep the house in order is broken down into how much time I need to get it done.

2. **I keep a healthy perspective.** Why am I doing it? To keep my wife happy and content with the fact that I have a different work schedule than she does.

This is a great place to explain the **Time/Effort Principle**. Please excuse my rambling as it may take a few pages, but it'll be worth it. I promise.

If you get a grip on this, time will go by with less stress. Both you and your wife will enjoy the benefits.

If you hate a task, view it as a time commitment with a definite end in mind. I'll finish in 10 minutes, and then it's done. Or in 30 minutes I won't have to do it again for another week.

Know how long it takes to complete a task and focus on the time.

Here's an example:

I hate yard work. Some people love it, but I hate it. Probably because, while growing up, I suffered from hay fever and my father insisted I mow the lawn.

It takes no more than 27 minutes to mow my current lawn. So I think, "After 27 minutes, it will be done for another week." That's a big motivation for me. That's a single sitcom I don't need to watch. That's less time than running a 5K, something my wife and I used to do together three times a week. (Yes, it takes us more than 30 minutes to run. We weren't fast, but we were consistent and healthier for doing it.)

When we moved into this house, we owned a riding lawn mower. We had a much bigger lawn at our previous home in North Carolina. But, the riding mower was overkill for this yard, so I sold the mower and hired someone to take care of the lawn for me. I had a regular job with a consistent income then, so paying someone else to do this job for me was no big deal. Now I wish we still had the riding mower. Oh well.

Looking back, I paid $15 per week for something I could do in less than 30 minutes. Put another way, that's $60 per month for less than 2 hours work.

Here's another example:

With too much unscheduled time and little self-discipline, I watched movies during the day. (Curse you, Netflix!) I don't do this anymore. I knew I had to clean the kitchen, but I didn't want to miss the movie I'd already seen at least a dozen times. (I love watching movies.) I'd break the kitchen work into small, doable tasks. Every commercial, I'd dash to the kitchen and do one of the jobs. It's amazing what you can do when you assign a specific length of time to complete one task. I can clean the stovetop in two commercial blocks, letting the cleaner sit for the required amount of time.

However, this doesn't work if you have HBO, Showtime, or Netflix. They don't have commercials. So get rid of the premium channels that cost extra. Save some money.

Time is the only resource we cannot hoard.

Since I have worked from home for the past four years, I have the time to do many things, as long as I do some advanced planning.

If I had a "real" job, I'd be working 40 hours a week, probably at a desk somewhere with typical hours and boring workloads. I'd come home bored and too emotionally drained to give much effort to anything else. This routine is easy for me to picture because it describes the job I had at a hospital for four years. Loved the people I worked with; hated the work.

But since I'm self-employed, I must control my own time, ensuring that I do the work I'm doing instead of watching reruns of NCIS or CSI. One thing I do give time to is volunteering.

For a while, I spent part of my week volunteering to roast coffee beans and serve as a barista at a local nonprofit coffee shop run by our church. I told you already. I'm a bit of a coffee snob.

Volunteering is either a luxury we indulge in to fill our time or something we find the time to do because we believe strongly in the cause.

Consider yourself primarily as a willing volunteer in the future of your marriage and family.

So, what are you volunteering/offering to your family?

- Your skills. Everybody has some skill they can give to a worthy cause. But to give your skill requires your time. I believe you have the time.

- Your effort. People are wiling to give more effort toward projects when they're passionate about them. A person will work 8 hours a day for a paycheck, 10-12 hours a day for a good boss, but 24 hours a day for a cause they're passionate about. But again, our effort is contingent on our available time. So be passionate about your family. Put effort into it.

- Your time: Let's take a closer look at this.

How much time do you have to give to your family if you have a regular job?

Let's do some math about your time:

- **How many hours in a week?**
  - 168 hours per week
- **Sleep:** 8 hours a night? (I wish.)
  - 8 x 7 = 56 hours of sleep per week
  - 168 – 56 = 112 waking hours per week

Are you with me so far? Good.

- **Let's say you work 40 hours a week.**
  - 112 – 40 = 72 waking, nonworking hours per week

- **Some daily quiet time.** Everybody needs this to stay healthy and focused. Half an hour a day is recommended, whether it is in prayer, meditation, or reading something uplifting. Add it as a non-negotiable time slot. Let's say, three hours a week.

  - 72 – 3 = 69 waking, free hours per week

- **Commute time.** According to a 2009 census, the average commute time is 25 minutes. Let's round that up to 30 minutes each way. That's 5 hours a week

  - 69 – 5 = 64 waking, free hours per week

- **What about preparing and eating food?** One hour a day sound about right? Might be low but let's go with it.

  - 64 – 7 = 57 waking, free hours per week

- **Household chores**. This time can vary. For husband or wives, time varies depending on the task at hand. Generally, women do a better job. If I'm stereotyping, I apologize. Let's go with 14 hours per week to keep things in immaculate order.

  - 57 – 14 = 43 waking, free hours per week

- **Family Time**. Whether you do it or not, I highly recommend this time frame: 1.5 hours per day. That's 10.5 hours per week. Round this up to 11. You can never spend too much time with your wife and kids.

  - 43 – 11 = 32 waking, free hours per week

What are we missing?

- **Finances.** One hour a week minimum.

- **Football (or some other show on TV, limited of course).** Three hours a week.

- **Exercise.** At least half an hour a day if you're healthy. So let's say 4 hours a week.

- **Hygiene.** Shower, shave, brush your teeth, hair (ladies), etc. The better part of an hour once you add it all up. That's seven more hours a week.

I'm ballparking these figures.

- Nevertheless 1 + 3 + 4 + 7 = 15

- Now 32 − 15 = 17

- **Your hobby.** That thing you love to do. One hour a day sounds about right on average, unless you're obsessed. Add another 7 hours a week.

- 17 − 7 = 10

WHERE DID ALL MY TIME GO?

Are you tired yet? I am. Now maybe add Internet surfing, twitter, Facebook. (Taking selfies and posting them.) Reading, writing, shopping, whatever.

- 10 − 10 = 0

But wait! I'm self-employed!

I still work 30 or so hours a week. If this is you, add 10 hours back into work time and the obvious lack of commute time (5 hours). Suddenly, you have well over 15 hours to take care of all the housework, cooking, cleaning, yard work (yuck), and whatever else you have to do. You're coming out on the right end of things.

NOTE: How much TV did I drop in there? Only three hours. For Americans, the average number is much higher. Oh well. For too many of us, this number is much higher than it ever needs to be and that sucks.

Before anyone gets all bent out of shape, let me stop you. This exercise is an idea (or ideal) of what some people's week may look like based on a few national averages as well as my personal opinion on some of it. So not very scientific. I get it.

Do your weekly time study right now. See how much time you spend, and how much time you have left. You spend your time wherever you choose.

Let's move forward.

All of my "Household Chores" fall into the following categories.

- Kitchen

- Cooking

- Laundry

- Yard Work

- Floors

- Errands

- Vehicles

- Random Stuff (There's always random stuff)

In doing all of these, I think of time, not effort. Why? Because I hate doing most of these things. I am not maintenance-oriented. Sorry, I already mentioned that. I do hate it.

So, here's how I deal with it all, using the **Time/Effort Principle**.

Kitchen

The countertops are picked up, the dishwasher is loaded/ unloaded, and the sink is clean. There are no piles of dirty anything around. The stovetop is clean (another big thing that bothers my wife), and generally, stuff is put away. These tasks takes me about 10 minutes a day. Ain't nothing.

Cooking

I am beginning to enjoy it. Some love it, but I'm not there yet. By planning ahead, it takes me no more than half an hour to make supper. I make enough supper for three. The third portion is my wife's lunch for work the next day. It saves time and keeps her on her chosen diet. I clean up after supper. Another 10 minutes. Before I go to bed, her breakfast, snack, and lunch are packed and ready for her. The coffee maker is primed and ready. And she loves me for doing this!

Laundry

I do this between other things. My wife makes a pile some-where. I get all the clothes into and out of the washer and dryer. Start a wash. Walk away (one-minute max). Later, put them in the dryer and start another load in the washer (two-minutes max). If there's a third time, fold from the dryer, new load in the dryer, and last load in the machine. The cycle for three loads: Wash. Wash/Dry. Wash/Dry/Fold. Dry/Fold. Fold. Timewise, that's one minute, two minutes, five minutes, four minutes, and three minutes, for a total of fifteen minutes over five stops to the laundry room. That's 15 minutes a week for all of it. Not bad, eh? I know what you're wondering, What about the ironing? (Yeah, right.) My wife prefers to do her own when she needs it. She knows I suck at it. I iron my clothing when needed. Most of the time she has to re-iron it for me.

Yard Work

I do it. Yuck. It takes 27 uninterrupted minutes to mow our yard—not 30 but 27. I'm that obsessive about it. Add another 15 minutes if I get the weed eater out. But I don't weed eat every week. If the sprinkler system has an issue, I deal with it at that time. Since I've planned and had the replacement parts that generally break on a regular basis, add another 30 minutes max.

Floors

Our floors are mostly hardwood with a little bit of carpet. The house is 2,200 square feet. Doing the floors is an absolute pain to me, almost like doing the yard, but I can't use rain as an excuse to put it off another day. A Swiffer Sweeper gets up most of the dust, followed by a hardwood floor spray and scrubber. (QUICK TIP: Take a shammy or Sham-Wow, cut it in quarters and use the pieces instead of the disposable Swiffer pads. Use both sides, wash, hang dry, repeat use. Saves a ton of money on those disposable ones.) The floors take more time than the lawn, around 40 minutes because I'm moving furniture around, etc. I use a steamer on the tile floors in the kitchen and bathrooms. Finally, I use a vacuum on the rug in the office and den. It's all done in less than an hour. Putting on headphones and listening to an audiobook or podcast helps the time go quicker and keeps me from getting bored. And when I get bored doing this stuff, I tend to speed up and do a lousy job.

Errands

Errands mainly consist of groceries. I go two times a week. The coffee shop where I spend most mornings during the week is next door to the grocery store. It's about 30 minutes at each stop, and no extra trips are needed. Why two trips? It just works better this way for me—fresher produce, etc. Because we're on a regular weekly plan for eating, the cost and the list is relatively simple. So around one hour a week. Easy.

Vehicles

I handle all of the maintenance for both vehicles. I even plan for filling up my wife's Honda as well. It's one less thing for her to deal with. It takes 10 minutes max, and she doesn't have to do it or worry about it. There have been times when Lisa will tell me at 9:00 p.m., "Oh, I'm out of gas." So I get it right then. It's no big deal for me. Yes, I wish I'd known sooner, but doing it when she informs me reinforces the idea that I'm willing to go out of my way to take care of something, so she doesn't have to worry about it. It's only 15 minutes or so. She'll get up in the morning with one less thing to worry about. I'm also getting better at asking her regularly if she needs a fill-up. Doing so keeps me from going out later at night. It also reinforces the idea that I'm taking care of her.

If you do your oil changes, that's no more than half an hour per vehicle every three months. If you take it somewhere, it usually takes longer, so have something with you to redeem the time while you wait.

Random

There's always something that comes up. Plan on an hour a week for "whatever it is." If you have to get her something she forgot, or whatever, just get it done.

The goal here is to keep the house in order for her sake. If it's not, she'll feel obligated to do it herself, which takes away from the free time she has. You want her to relax when she's home. You want her to see her time at home as free time. The only way for her to feel like that is to know she doesn't have to do very much when she gets home.

By the way, the dog is another story. I'm the one who does the daily walking (30-45 minutes), the regular training when she was a pup (20-30 minutes) and the feeding/cleaning/activity that comes with having a dog. It's a good thing I love dogs.

Even with all of this stuff, including the dog, (5 days per week, liberally rounding up)

- Kitchen: One half hour

- Cooking: One hour including cleanup

- Laundry: One half hour

- Yard Work: One hour

- Floors: One hour

- Errands: One and a half hours

- Vehicles: One hour

- Random: One Hour

Total

It takes 7½ hours per week to keep the house in order.

If you're working 40 hours a week, you may have to find a way to squeeze some of this stuff into your schedule. No one says you have to do all of these activities. But adding just one more thing to your list is one less thing on your wife's list. Your loved one will notice and be happy you do it. That's not bad. If you do it right, that's a win/win situation, and your wife will feel like you're doing so much more.

What about me? What about my free time?

I know this is what you're thinking. You work hard. You need some time for yourself. So far, it seems like all you're reading is, "Do all of the work and let your wife kick back and relax."

Realize the following:

- If you were alone, you'd be doing all of these things anyway. Right?

- This is what I do. Doing all of this may not be possible or realistic for you and your family schedule. I get that. Adapt this information to fit you.

- It is possible for you to do more than you're doing now. Adapt my suggestions to your situation.

- Share the load between the two of you. If there are children in your life, great. Teach them household responsibility at an early age.

- No one is telling you to do all of this alone. The goal is to take ownership of the home. Take the lead and don't just expect your spouse to do most of it. If you take ownership of one thing your spouse regularly does and make it your own. Then you've accomplished the goal of this chapter.

- Communicate. To get the house in order, so to speak, sit down with your wife and get on the same page regarding whatever has to get done. You may need to do this weekly because your schedules may change weekly. Ours does. A little communication saves a lot of misunderstanding and headaches.

- THE KEY: When you take the lead in taking care of the home, its maintenance and workflow, your wife will appreciate it. She will feel loved because of your initiative in this area.

THIS IS THE POINT!

Someone has to take the lead. It needs to be you. Just adopting this attitude will increase your household productivity and ease your spouse's stress a little. Great job.

Being together with household details can give your business efforts a productive boost.

I've read many different articles regarding productivity and scheduling. Several gurus on the topic suggest working for 50-minute time blocks and taking ten minutes of rest. That may work for some people, but not for me. It is an individualistic thing.

When I'm focused on something, I go at it for several hours. Nothing could get me away from the task at hand. Right now, for instance, I'm in a coffee shop. I've taken away the distractions of home and dog. As soon as I slow down, I grab another cup of coffee or eat my breakfast. I've been here since 6:30 a.m. after walking from home, which is a mile away. I won't leave until noon.

When I get home, I have a list of things to do around the house. Everything gets done.

However, I don't walk to the coffee shop every day. When I work from home, I close the door to the office so the dog can't demand my attention. I come out for regular breaks. I toss the ball off the back porch. I clean up the kitchen. I start a load of wash. In my short, planned breaks, I find a rhythm between rest from work and doing little things around the house. Usually, I take an hour or so in the afternoon to get some chores done. Cooking always sneaks in there as well.

Unless you, as an entrepreneur, can find balance between your work at home and working from home, your marriage will struggle. You can make it work. Take full advantage of your schedule. Kill the distractions. Plan your transitions. When you do, you will be amazed at how much you can get done in both worlds.

MASTER FINANCIAL UNITY

*No one's ever achieved financial fitness with a January
resolution that's abandoned by February.*
Suze Orman

*Money won't create success,
the freedom to make it will.*
Nelson Mandela

Secret #6:
A balanced budget takes equal effort.

While Lisa and I worked hard at loving and listening to each other to rebuild our marriage, she decided what she wanted to do with her life—become a nurse.

Do you know how much a youth pastor made at a small church back in the mid-'80s? Next to nothing, that's how much. Mind you; I wasn't complaining back then. They provided our housing. So, we had that going for us.

We couldn't afford college payments. Neither of us had a clue about financial aid, but when she started pursuing the idea, grants were available. She became a nurse with no expense to our fragile income status. Yay.

While she went off to school, my time taking care of the house increased and hers decreased. When she saw how supportive I was of her career efforts, our marriage grew stronger than ever. Still, we had to keep tight reigns on the finances.

Way back in our second year of life together, I was working in Ohio at a church. Sadly, it just wasn't working out at all. I'd been there only eight months. Lisa had a job making a whopping $80 a week. I walked into the church one Monday morning, and the Senior Pastor called me into his office.

"Your services here are no longer required. Here's a check for $1,000. You have the morning to clear out your office. I'm sorry it didn't work out for all of us."

Now, let's do the math. Our rent was $250 a month. (Yay for the good old '80s.) My wife was making how much again? $80 a week. I had a check that would get us through four months' rent. What were we going to do?

We had two options. First was to hit up our parents for a bailout loan. That'd be great, but it wouldn't solve the problem in the long run.

The second was to tell no one at all. We'd pray about it. Pray and trust God.

It was one of the hardest things we ever did as a couple. Together, we trusted God with the most tangible part of our lives: our finances.

I cast out some resumes and left it at that. Three and a half months into this free fall experiment of faith, Lisa came home and told me she'd lost her job—not what I was expecting to hear. That same week, I got a call from a church in North Carolina. Three weeks later, we were off on a new adventure, a new job, and the near death of our marriage. Three years after that was the seventh year itch that almost split us for good.

Fortunately, we'd learned from earlier experience that finances were something never to take for granted. Our crumbling and rebuilding marriage efforts made us even more aware of our need for God's guidance in finances and relationships. Had we allowed finances to be a matter of dispute in our marriage, it could have been the straw that broke the camel's back. Thankfully, it did not.

We stayed in North Carolina for 16 years. We rebuilt our marriage but still never made a ton of money. Our best financial decision as a couple was Lisa's passion for becoming a nurse.

All that to say this: Make sure your finances are in order before venturing out into the entrepreneurial world. Immediate success takes years.

Fast forward through the next 16 years, and beyond, where we enjoy living in Colorado.

When we moved here in 2000, we bought a home built in 1971. It had a hot tub on the back deck. I thought it'd be great. Our daughter loved it more than we did.

She used it regularly until she went off to university. We kept it hot but never used it much. Chemicals were pricey, but we maintained it for more than two years, using it no more than half a dozen times.

I guess we liked the idea of having a hot tub more than using it.

By hot tub standards, ours was not huge—only 375 gallons of water. When it started having electrical issues, it'd cost us over $100 to get a "Hot Tub Tech" out to fix it. After doing that a few times, I unplugged it and drained it. Without having to keep the water hot, our electric bill went down about $34 a month. That is significant savings.

At coffee shops, I switched from specialty coffee drinks to just straight coffee, which saved around $6 a week.

I cut back on my snacks and saved around $7 every time I went to the grocery store.

Like just about every family, you go through financially hard times.

You nickel & dime yourself to death due to small, needless spending habits.

I am the master of the Nickel & Dime Budget Kill. A coffee here and a pastry there—it all adds up.

Sadly, here's a sample of my week if I don't watch everything I spend:

- Coffee Shop: 3 visits, 3 coffees at $2.00 each plus a cinnamon roll or toasted bagel at least once at $2.44. So, $8.44 a week

- Groceries: An extra snack just about every time I pick something up which is twice per week. So, $3.00 x 2 = $6.00 or so.

- Eat out at least once per week by myself, which I really don't need to do. $7.50.

- Impulse snack: $1.50

- On Demand movie on cable: $6.99 (2x/month)

Add it all up:

- $8.44 + $6.00 + $7.50 + $1.50 = $23.44 per week

- $23.44 x 4 weeks = $93.76 per month

- $6.99 x 2 = $13.98 per month

- $93.76 + $13.98 = $107.74 per month

STOP IT!
JUST STOP WASTING MONEY!
(I'm yelling at myself)

The point of this short chapter is simple.

Whether you are the one tracking the budget or your wife is, it doesn't matter. You value her income, your income, and the family finances, by being the guy who is careful and calculated when spending money to get your "independent project" off the ground.

I admit it. I am the worst person in the world to write advice on saving money. I am the worst at saving money, but I am learning.

I defer most of my needed knowledge to my sources and give you a little advice from personal experience and failure. **NOTE:** Maybe your wife is the financial genius in the family. That's great. That puts you in an even better position to ease her stress and make her feel more secure and loved. You'll see what I mean eventually.

So let me throw at you what I've adopted, as the worst financial husband ever, but also the one who keeps track of the finances for our family. Yes, I'm the one who does it. It's one less thing for my wife to worry about.

Track every penny

Here's what happens if you don't:

- You will never be able to stick to a budget.

- You will wonder where all your money went.

- Your wife will wonder why she is working so hard, and you have no clue where it all went.

- You'll end up having to get a second part-time job to make end meet, earning no more than you waste on stuff you don't need.

Here's what happens when you do:

- You will become accountable to both yourself and your wife.

- Your eyes will be opened as to how much of your money you waste.

- You will become more responsible when you open your wallet or make a discretionary purchase.

- You will think twice before you buy that new replacement pocketknife that costs too much. (Oh, sorry. That was me. You'd never do anything like that.)

Know exactly what income you'll have every month

This past August, I knew that my wife would get paid three times. She didn't do any extra work. That's just how her paychecks fell. For that month, she received paychecks on the 2nd, the 16th, and the 30th.

If you're working by a monthly budget, this is good news. If you've planned, use this money for savings, projects, investments, a rainy day fund, emergency fund, and so on.

If your family income is discretionary, based on how many hours worked, look at your income for the past 10 to 12 months. If your income is a variable, like mine is, then look at your spouse's income only and add your least profitable month. Create a budget based on the steadiest income only. See what is possible before making any decisions on budget items.

Don't keep up with the Joneses. They're idiots anyway.

Life is not a competition. You don't have to keep up with anybody. Be proud that you don't have your neighbor's car payment.

Aside: What is your car? A status symbol? A lifestyle? Basic reliable transportation? Do you need all those bells and whistles? Are they essential? Probably not. Just saying.

The Joneses are an illusion. They may have a good public appearance, but they may also be just a paycheck or two away from serious financial ruin. Define your lifestyle; don't copy someone else's.

Resources

I recommend two financial resources that I have personal experience with. I'm sure there are tons more, but I've learned that gathering too many resources can bottleneck your actions. Get one plan going. Adjust that plan to your style without losing the integrity of the program itself. Then, keep at it. Work the plan.

Financial Peace

My first recommendation is Financial Peace University, Dave Ramsey's bread and butter product. It has changed the lives of many families when it comes to financial wisdom.

Dave is the master of mastering your money in every aspect of the term. You may not agree with everything he has to say, but he has a ton of good practical concepts on saving money. His website can get you started on creating a simple budget. His books are extremely practical and easy to understand so anyone can get started. Reading his free online resources will direct you to any books he has available, and there are many. Be choosy.

Mint.com

This is a free online resource that tracks your spending. One of the many features I like is you can view your information on your smartphone. You can check your spending daily. Set it up online, including your budget. If you trust them with your financial info (I did), then you can get up-to-date info on your spending habits. Since it's free, you'll have to put up with a few ads and "recommendations" to invest in a few things. I ignore them for the most part.

With a little research, you can find more resources to inform and enlighten you regarding your spending/saving habits and how to adjust them. Use whatever you wish, but don't go overboard by spending too much to begin saving. It may be counter-productive. You gotta start somewhere. So start already.

I understand that this chapter may not apply to most couples. If you're the couple that has a firm grip on your finances, that's great. Good for you. Keep it up.

Personal story. This'll scare you to death. It did me.

Back in the mid-2000s, I received an inheritance from my mother's estate—$50,000, to be exact. I didn't want to let the money sit, so I decided to get involved in the stock market.

You know where this is going already, don't you?

Trading small stocks, I made about $10,000. Wow! Was I ever confident. I jumped into day-trading stock options. Within the next two years, I lost it all and then some.

When I had a good day, I'd tell my wife, and she'd be so proud of me. I felt good. On bad days, I wouldn't tell her a thing. There were more bad days than good ones.

When I finally lost it all, I had to tell her. It was one of the worst days of my life. To my amazement and salvation, my wife was quick to forgive my stupidity. We moved on. She's amazing.

It was then I decided to honor the family, and her hard-earned income and mine, by taking a personal interest in spending less, taking fewer chances, and making my wife feel safer and more secure because I was careful with our financial future.

You would do well to do the same. Your wife will love you for it.

If your outgo exceeds your income, your upkeep will be your downfall.

Being financially responsible may be a no-brainer to some. But it isn't to everybody.

Being Together with your finances ensures business longevity.

There is a part of our family budget specific to my business. I don't make enough to support the family fully. My wife, however, is blessed with a decent salary for her skills and passion.

I have to be honest with you. I have spent money and blown the budget by jumping into an educational offer to further my online efforts. I've done so without telling her. Yikes. If she reads this part of the book, I'll have some explaining to do.

I'm okay with that, and I'll tell you why. To some extent, the end justifies the means. The means, in this case, was spending extra money. The end is a better business overall.

Now, there are many fantastic offers out there to "further my online education." If I did this with every one, we'd be broke. I'm very selective. You need to be as well.

Recently, received a free phone consultation with an amazing man who develops brand creation and business focus. His 15-minute free time with me ended up being an hour. We enjoyed each other's company, and his insights were beneficial.

His sales pitch at the end of our time was low key. That's just his style. I would spend two full days with him, one-on-one. We'd meet at his home, go through tons of material explicitly tailored for where I am and the business needs I currently have. My wife would come along. It would be specific and personal. He has recorded results and testimonials that fully justify the cost.

The price tag: $5,000.

I'd never even attempt to hide this expense from my wife. I could because I handle the finances in the family. But, there comes the point, a line in the sand, where you sit down with your wife and have a talk about the opportunity.

You may have the money, but the timing isn't right. It may be the right timing for your business, but the money would be real tight. You have to be together on these decisions. If the opportunity puts too much strain on the family, the price is too high.

Lisa and I are praying over the opportunity, both separately and as a couple. We'll see where it leads. Fortunately, there is no deadline for this offer. Revisiting it in six months may be the right thing to do. Jumping in this month may result in a positive return on investment within six months. Decisions like this hard. Praying together helps clarify the process.

CONQUER YOUR FUTURE TOGETHER

*You cannot escape the responsibility of tomorrow
by evading it today.*
Abraham Lincoln

*Life is divided into three terms—that which was,
which is, and which will be. Let us learn from the past
to profit by the present, and from the present,
to live better in the future.*
William Wordsworth

Secret #7:
Support her path and
she'll love yours more.

Lisa and I weathered the seventh year storm that was our failing marriage. The more we worked at getting ourselves together, the more we saw ourselves as two rails taking the same train someplace special. The tracks never cross each other. They don't get closer either. They do stay together, head in the same direction, and represent two different people committed to each other.

I'm no longer in church ministry. Lisa is no longer a nurse. I give my primary time to her, and in turn, I get hers. I'm writing, speaking and developing an online business. She went on to get a Master's degree as a family nurse practitioner.

I had a Plan A for my career. After a long successful career in one field, I'd retire with a fantastic retirement plan.

Well, that has not happened, and it never will. I found myself creating my career instead of relying on an organization to do it for me.

In 2012, *Forbes Magazine* wrote an article titled, "Job Hopping Is the 'New Normal' for Millennials." It highlighted the Human Resources nightmare of this reality. I'm not a millennial, but I have changed jobs and jumped industries several times.

In another article by *Career Advice Online*, it begins "Career change statistics suggest that the average person will be making a career change approximately 5-7 times during their working life."

I've been a cheese maker, maintenance technician, youth pastor, youth and music pastor, (that one was a stretch for me), program coordinator in a hospital, transportation supervisor for a behavioral health unit, and a volunteer barista at a non-profit coffee shop. I enjoyed that last one. I love coffee. Now I'm an author and working on my own online business. One career? Not me. Probably not you either.

When I planned to marry Lisa 38+ years ago, my Plan A for the marriage was to marry once and make it last a lifetime. The problem with my Plan A was that one single sentence was too simplistic.

I got the "marry once" part down. We both said, "I do" in front of 300 people. The "make it last" part had no legs to it and no direction to head toward. I thought it would happen all by itself.

I thought the Plan A would materialize as time went on. I couldn't have been more wrong.

It didn't happen that way. I had to get a kick in the head, and that kick came from my wife.

Seven years into our marriage, my Plan A job was in high gear. My marriage was almost in the toilet. She almost left me.

Thankfully, she came back. She gave me another chance to be the husband she knew I could be. She came home, and I changed. We changed. I learned to give more time, effort, and attention to her needs. Everything changed.

I discovered that I could still do my job well, and give my wife what she needed in our marriage. Whew.

I know I already told you this story. I started the book with this, didn't I? It bears repeating because I've worked very hard to keep my marriage. It has been the single most rewarding use of time ever spent.

When she first told me she was thinking about not coming back, so many things flashed through my mind. How can I be a divorced youth pastor? How can I be effective in my work without her? How can I go on without her? How can I live without her?

The thoughts kept escalating. The very idea of losing her scared me to death.

She meant so much to me, and yet I was oblivious to what she needed from me. Whoever said "Love is blind" never mentioned the husband being blind to the needs of the one he's planning to live with for the rest of his life.

I thought there was one reason why she came back. I doubt my begging was the sole reason. No, she came back because she always keeps her word. She is honest and committed. She also saw there was still hope for us. Her belief in keeping her commitments helped her see there was hope in me. Hope for us. Commitment and hope brought her back. She might tell you something different, but that's how she made me see it. When she came back, I saw hope for our future.

I took the concept of the husband as the leader of the relationship personally and literally. By doing so, I diminished her role in the marriage. After my wakeup call, I promised I would never take our marriage for granted ever again.

Marriage doesn't just happen. It is hard work that is extremely rewarding. Over time, the "work" of marriage becomes less like work and more like joy.

So, if you're going to take ownership of your marriage success from this day forward, you need a plan—a deliberate, calculated plan.

Read the following statements from women regarding their husbands found at this website: HTTP://marriagebuilders.com/graphic/mbi8111_ leave.html

"I hurt all the time because I feel alone and abandoned."
"My husband is no longer my friend."
"The only time he pays attention to me is when he wants sex."
"He is never there for me when I need him the most."
"When he hurts my feelings he doesn't apologize."
"He lives his life as if we weren't married; he rarely considers me."
"We're like ships passing in the night, he goes his way and I go mine."
"My husband has become a stranger to me, I don't even know who he is anymore."
"He doesn't show any interest in me or what I do."

Okay, these statements scare me. Do they scare you? They should.

Can you envision your wife saying one of these statements about you? Which one is it?

Consider it your wakeup call. It's time to do something about it.

Being together and looking forward together guarantees long-term happiness in both marriage and business.

To start a new business of any kind without a business plan is a recipe for failure. I know because I started my marriage with a business plan that left my wife out of the equation. I've also started this concept of having an online business without any clear direction and have restarted it several times. Thankfully, I've finally settled in with a specific course.

It's a process. Marriage and business are a process. Processes take lots of work. It requires adjustment. It takes cooperation.

You need a plan:

- That excites you.

- You can follow through on.

- You can commit to.

- That won't bankrupt you.

- That convinces your spouse you haven't given up and never will.

- That builds confidence back into the marriage.

- That is feasible, doable, and not overwhelming.

- That will keep you happily married for the rest of your lives.

So, here's a plan for you to adopt and adapt to suit your own situation.

Step #1: Lose The Excuses

"It's her fault."
"She is not physically available for me."
"She won't listen to me when I talk to her."
"We hardly ever see each other anymore."
"She's too busy with her career."
"She is not the same person I married."

Add your excuses to this list. I know you have some. Get it out of your system.

NOW, lose the excuses, which are a way to justify not doing something yourself. You're passing the blame off on your wife. Stop it.

It's never one person's fault in a struggling marriage. There is a good argument for placing some blame on both sides.

Stop coming up with excuses for not making an effort to make your marriage better than it is right now.

Oh, and don't play the "Blame Game" either. Don't point the finger at your loved one. It's never all their fault, and it's never all your fault. To get from where you are to where you'd like to be, someone has to take the initiative and move in that direction. That person is you.

Step #2: Make A List

There's a ton of things you can do right now to implement the many suggestions given to you in the previous pages. But not all of them are going to work for your situation.

Bear in mind that I work from home and on my schedule. There's a good chance you do not.

So, make a list of at least ten things you can feasibly do— things that work for your situation and your circumstances.

For example, we have one child. She's 25 and lives in Guatemala for ten months out of the year. Nothing I've written so far includes kids. Therefore, I have more time on my hands than the family with three kids under the age of ten.

This is why you need a list—your list, not mine.

- Your list must be actions that will fit into your regular schedule, so you don't get overwhelmed.

- Your list must be specific to you and your spouse. Both of you are unique in personality, circumstances, and present situations (work, home, kids, etc.), so your list has to be unique as well.

- Your list is nobody else's business. Not even your wife's. Let her make her list.

- Your list must be spread out over several areas of your lives together, e.g., ten little things that all have to do with one aspect of your marriage makes it too one-dimensional. It can be too easily misinterpreted as having an ulterior motive. You don't want it to go that way.

- Your list should have practical items (taking out the garbage without being asked), social items (holding hands when your spouse least expects you to), spiritual items (pray with her before she leaves the house), personal items (compliment her on something you've never praised before), and so on. Be diverse.

  - ○ ______________________________________

  - ○ ______________________________________

  - ○ ______________________________________

  - ○ ______________________________________

○ _________________________________

○ _________________________________

○ _________________________________

○ _________________________________

○ _________________________________

○ _________________________________

Step #3: Pick One Thing And Own It

In the previous pages, you gleaned at least two dozen ideas you can use to kick-start your marriage. Don't try to do them all at once, which will overwhelm you. Not only that, it'd probably shock your spouse to death.

Decide to do one thing that would work best for your situation.

- Pick something just beyond the ordinary.

- Pick something she would never expect you to do.

- Pick something you can repeat regularly.

The goal is that no matter where you are in your marriage, you want it to be better than it is. It starts with one simple step, one action on your part to make it better.

Here's the very first thing for you to do, and it is the key to everything else you should plan to do.

Pray:

- To be a better husband.

- To be more attentive.

- To have no other motive than to be a better guy for her.

- To meet her needs—her needs, not yours.

- For and support your wife's spiritual growth.

- To be the husband she will want to love, because of your overwhelming love for her.

- For her to be open and receptive to your efforts.

- For your own direction to be clear as you dive into this challenge.

Once you do that, pick one thing that will start it all off, and own it.

Step #4: Pick Up The Pace A Little

So you started holding hands again after all these years. Good for you. (Why did you ever stop?)

Your wife is receptive to a few changes in your life when it comes to your marriage together. Fantastic.

Now, what else are you going to do? Well, you've got your list of ten things. Maybe there are a few things you can add.

Wait! You've not done all ten yet? That's okay. Once you start thinking this way and doing a few things, new ideas will come to mind. DON'T LOSE THESE NEW IDEAS. Write them down. Record them somewhere.

I keep a running list on my cell phone in a notes app. If you're like I am, a great idea can come and go in a few seconds. Do whatever you can to capture those ideas. Review them regularly. Decide what might work, or realize the great idea you had last week in the grocery store is just idiotic. Edit your list accordingly.

Step #5: Pick The Brains Of Other Husbands

Ask your friends this question, "What's one thing you do for your wife regularly that makes her feel special?"

Some may come up with an immediate answer. Great. Maybe it'll work in your marriage: maybe it won't. Keep the thought for possible adaptation. You never know.

If your friend can't think of anything, that's a great discussion starter. Plan to have a suggestion or two to share with him.

Try this exercise right now

Think of your best friend's marriage. (I assume he is married and their marriage is doing great. It is as far as you know.) What are three things they do that you don't do in your marriage? Write them down.

- ____
- ____
- ____

Can you adapt and implement one of these in your marriage? How? When?

NOTE: Don't copy someone else's situation. Your astute wife may notice the "copycat" appearance. So, timing and adaptation are key to a good idea.

Step #6: Expect Some Actions To Be Bombs And Duds

You may be excited about making the bed every morning for her. (Maybe not.) You may be thrilled to surprise your wife by taking her to that new restaurant. You may be pumped to get her that neat new gift.

BUT...

What if you make the bed all wrong for her liking? (Yeah, this happens. Believe me. You know what I mean.)

What if she hates Tex-Mex, there's nothing on the menu she likes, the whole evening is a bust, and you're both still hungry?

What if she opens the present with a preconceived idea and finds you got her funky earrings you think she'll love, but she thinks are ugly? (I bought my wife a necklace on Fifth Ave in NYC in the lobby of one of Trump's buildings. Got a fantastic deal on it, or else I wouldn't have bought it at all. I gave it to her with high expectations she would love it and wear it weekly. It's been over eight years, and I've yet to see it around her neck. Oh well.)

There will be duds. Bombs. Oops. Blew that one. Whatever.

And these bombs may leave your spouse scratching her head thinking, "What was that? Has my husband lost his mind?"

It's okay. Ever hear of Ed Delahanty? Me neither. He's fifth on the list of all-time professional baseball players who got at least three out of ten hits in a career batting average (.3458 to be exact). And this was over a 15-year career. Yup, he's in the Hall of Fame. Crazy for a man who struck out at least four times out of every ten. He had a lot of duds. He's still a great player that almost nobody remembers.

Your marriage isn't baseball, but it's crazy to think you can hit a fair ball every time. Ed couldn't. You have to keep swinging. Keep stepping up to the plate. Keep thinking of more baseball analogies to add to this paragraph.

The point

Keep trying. Keep doing something and making an effort. It will be worth it in the long run. It will result in a better marriage.

Step #7: There Is No Ulterior Motive

In the previous pages, you probably had this thought:

"Will doing these things get me more sex with my wife?"

Wow, typing that seems so selfish and one-sided. But you thought this, didn't you? Admit it. We are all human. And, yes, I've thought about this as well. Probably more than I should.

However, if this is one of your main motives, then stop right now. Your marriage is worth so much more than sex.

Read the following words out loud, unless you're currently in a coffee shop.

You don't work hard at having great sex, hoping it will lead to a great marriage.

Great sex in a marriage is the result of working hard at having a great marriage.

I write this with no apologies whatsoever. This is not a guarantee, but if I were a betting man, I'd put money on this, lots and lots of money.

However, if this is your primary motive, your wife will know. You can't hide an incentive like this. It's impossible. (Women can sense this motive miles away and days before it arrives. I kid you not.)

If you implement one or twenty ideas suggested in this book over the next year or so, and your marital sex life doesn't increase at all, so what? You've still got a better marriage because of your efforts. Your wife will love you more than ever. You win. Your wife wins. Your marriage wins.

I used to buy my wife flowers regularly. She loved them. In a few days they'd begin to wilt, and eventually, they would die. Spending $60 for 4-5 days isn't a good use of money.

But she loved them. They were gorgeous. My thoughtfulness in taking the time and money to get them for her meant more to her than the flowers themselves.

However, for her to have fresh flowers regularly means I'd have to get her flowers all the time. Pretty soon, it isn't special. It's expected.

She will appreciate it more if you practice any of these simple suggestions regularly than buying flowers every six months or so. Flowers are a Band-Aid on a gaping wound. It just doesn't work long-term.

DISCLAIMER: My wife loves getting flowers, but I don't buy them very often. She knows why. She expects fewer flowers from me, and I do surprise her now and then. I hate spending money on flowers, but she loves to get them. So, there's that.

Back to the list. No, the list is not in this book. It's my list. I'll let you check it out if you wish. You can call it "Your Starter List." Take each item, adapt, toss, rewrite, whatever. Make your list.

If you purchased the book within the first three to four days of publication, the list was part of your bonus material. Lucky you.

Oh, One Last Thing Or Two

Don't let your wife know you're following this tremendous new plan you found in a book. It may come across as a little canned or cheesy. Then again, so what?

Don't tell your wife to read this book unless she was the one who found it and gave it to you. In that case, no doubt, she's already skimmed it. (If she did buy it, say thank you and don't make a big deal out of it.)

If you don't do a single thing suggested in this book, at least do something. Accepting the status quo in any marriage creates a dying marriage.

Cultivate, Plant, Water, Repeat

I realize that most of this book and all the ideas are from the perspective of a married couple with no children, or, in our case, one grown child no longer living at home.

- Maybe you have three kids under the age of five, like good friends of ours, heaven help them.

- Maybe you have two teenagers and a ten-year-old. Lord, have mercy on your souls!

If this is the case, you may have read this book thinking, this guy is crazy and out of touch with my whole world, or reality in general. I assure you, I am not. This is my reality. Make yours better. Do it with some of the ideas and suggestions you read.

If you have children at home, you as a husband need to make every effort to be the best husband you can be.

Your kids are watching you. They see how you treat each other. They feel how you treat each other. They watch how you fight. They see how you make up. They know how special you are to each other. They observe how you're making an effort, or not making any effort at all.

Don't kid yourself. Your children see, feel, and sense all of this. And what are they doing with this modeled information from you, their parents?

- They're learning how to love their future mate.

- They're learning how to communicate.

- They're learning how to fight and argue.
- They're learning how to make up.
- They're learning how to pay attention.
- They're learning how to ignore each other.
- They're learning how to adjust.
- They're learning how to give.
- They're learning how to take.
- They're learning how to surprise each other.
- They're learning how to stay in love.
- They're learning what commitment really means.
- They're learning what it means to "finish what you start."
- They're learning the meaning of affection.
- They're learning what it means to support each other's dreams.
- They're learning the art of compromise.
- They're learning that it takes more than one to make a marriage work.
- They're learning that they're loved more when they give more.

Yes, they're learning all of this and so much more.

So, if you feel that most of this book and all of its suggestions won't work for you, I'm okay with that. BUT, you have to do something. You have to try something. You have to make a continued effort at making your marriage more blissful than it already is.

You have to start the process. I don't care how good your marriage is. It won't stay that way. There is ebb and flow. There are smooth times and rough times. Be prepared for both.

Your effort (or lack of effort) does not go unnoticed. Your kids are watching. So are your neighbors, but who cares what they think.

The greatest gift you can give your children is the model of a godly, loving marriage.

6 HABITS TO KEEP YOUR MARRIAGE ON TRACK

Our character is basically a composite of our habits.
Because they are consistent, often unconscious patterns,
they constantly, daily, express our character.
Stephen Covey

You will never change your life until you change some-
thing you do daily.
John Maxwell

Secret #8:
What you do daily IS the difference.

My marriage was almost history. My wife almost left me. She called me from another country to say she was thinking about never coming back to me. We'd been married for seven years at the time. I thought everything was fine. I could not have been more wrong.

She was trying to pull my head out of the sand because I was completely buried in doing everything but having a great marriage. Having an okay marriage is the worst thing you can have, for a least one of you.

Here are the six habits I added to my life to keep the love of my life for the rest of my life. Adopt these habits in your life, and you'll be married forever. Seriously, this is a good thing.

1. Intentionally listen.

It is so easy to tune out whatever your spouse says when you assume he/she doesn't have something important to say. Stop it. Close the computer, mute the TV, set down the iPad, and listen. If you physically and intentionally do this, it tells your spouse that you believe they have something important to say, and you don't want to miss it. Even if it's about shoes.

2. Never Multitask.

"I'm listening, dear. I'm just doing this one thing as well." When you stop doing one thing to fully engage in whatever your spouse is doing or saying, you tell him/her they are more important than anything you happen to be doing at that time. Be singularly focused on her when she needs it.

3. Give a Daily Kiss or Two.

I'm serious. You must kiss your spouse at least once a day. I have a daily habit of kissing my wife goodbye every morning before she leaves for work—every day without fail. She leaves knowing that I love her. Kissing her is the first thing I do when I get into bed at night (or when she gets into bed, whichever one gets in last.) I initiate this. Doing this tells your wife you love her.

4. Initiate Physical Touch.

Not touching your spouse in an affectionate way every day is never recommended. Wait? What about that kiss? That doesn't count. I purposefully give my wife a hug, a squeeze, a pat on the _____ at least once a day, regardless.

5. Be Over Encouraging.

You get excited about different things than your spouse. You are different people. Recognize your spouse's interests and aspirations and start encouraging. Be the cheerleader. Sure, be realistic. Sometimes you have to keep your spouse grounded in reality. Work together to keep the truth intact without jumping off the deep end.

6. Never Attach Strings to Anything.

There are no strings attached to anything on the list above. Never think that if you start doing #3, #4, and #5 every day that it will lead to a more amorous ending. That is not the motive. It can be a great benefit, but it's not the eventual goal. You do all these things intentionally without any assumptions. Do this and see where it leads.

When my wife told me she was thinking about leaving me, I begged, literally begged, her to give me one last chance. I promised to change. I vowed to do anything to make our marriage work. She gave me one last shot. I kept my promises. I changed. I did everything I could to make our marriage better. And because I did it, we changed. When I changed, she changed. We changed together. We grew together.

We're still changing, adjusting, and tweaking our marriage. We never give up on each other, even after 35 years. Especially after 35 years.

What are you doing regularly to keep your marriage solid?

YOUR FIRST NEXT STEP

In doing everything, from coming up with the ideas and putting them on paper till doing the final edits, you are always thinking the next three steps, you're always think- ing what next, what next, what next?
Andrew McCarthy

The secret to success, to parenting, to life, is to not count up the cost. Don't focus on all the steps it will take. Don't stare into the abyss at the giant leap it will take. That view will keep you from taking the next small step.
Regina Brett

Secret #9:
You'll figure out the rest once you start but you have to start.

My young wife came back home from her week away. She didn't go off with her high school sweetheart. I guess that's obvious now.

Yes, I know. I've said this too many times already. I'm the luckiest man on the planet. Because she did, I'm also one of the happiest.

Our next several months together included many of the suggestions written in this book. Some things took me years to figure out. I figured them out because I became obsessed with making my wife happy. This was the best thing I could have done. You would be wise to take the same path.

I haven't made the following claim before now, but both my wife and I firmly agree that it's completely true. Here goes.

Separation and divorce in any marriage is NEVER just one person's fault.
No one is completely innocent.
No one is completely guilty.
It takes two to tango, even if the tango is a mess.

So, I don't care where your marriage is right now. If it's 100% fantastic, then congratulations are in order. Both of you had something to do with that. If it's 99% in the toilet, then both of you had something to do with that as well. It is never just one person's fault.

If you can't admit this, toss this book out and get a lawyer. However, I believe you can acknowledge you had your hand in creating a "less-than-ideal" marriage. I know this because you're almost finished reading this book.

Sure, you can argue that it's more her fault than your fault, which may even be true. But throwing blame around gets you nowhere. It only clouds things up even more.

Stop taking on the world of platform building, achieving online domination, and creating the business of your dreams if doing so is slowly (or quickly) killing your marriage. It's okay to go at it a little slower as long as your wife comes along for the ride.

I've read about many people who rose to online dominance and created a fantastic career for themselves and their families. Some rose quickly. Some took to it naturally. Others have struggled and kept at it. I've taken my time. I could do more, but I'm having too much fun taking care of my wife.

Now, if you just skipped the first nine chapters of this book because the Table of Contents said Chapter 10 was titled "Next Steps," then go back to the Table of Contents and start reading every page, every word. This book is not that long, but it's full of practical stuff you can use. Shortcuts don't give you the whole picture. Marriage shortcuts will end in a short marriage. You can quote me on that.

There are no shortcuts to a great marriage. Marriage is hard work for two people, not just one. You have to learn how to live together. You have to learn how the person you love loves you.

The great thing is that two people are working hard on one big project. That project is your marriage, and you want it to last a lifetime.

With that in mind, here are four foundational truths that Lisa and I used as we began to rebuild our marriage.

Shut up and listen

When Lisa came home, I had to get her to share with me what she was feeling and what led her to consider leaving me forever. So it began with me shutting up.

Too many people think that communication has to do with how one person transfers information to another person. This is wrong. Everybody wants the other person to understand him or her.

I'm with Stephen Covey on this. Habit #5 of his book, *The 7 Habits Of Highly Effective People*, is to seek first to understand, then to be understood.

I had to get my wife to talk to me and share her feelings, which was no easy task. But, she was willing to try to save our marriage, just as I was. She opened up, and I shut up. I didn't argue her points, right or wrong. I didn't get defensive. Okay, I tried hard not to get defensive, but I kept it inside. I had to shut up and listen.

Never once did I think about leaving her, but she thought long and hard about leaving me. I hurt her more than I ever realized.

My wife told me it was at least three years into our marriage before she ever won an argument with me. Most of the time, she'd concede to my arrogance just to shut me up. Apparently, I'm good at arguing. (Not something to brag about.) When she finally did win her first argument, the event was so significant to her that she announced the victory out loud. Until she mentioned this, I never noticed. Why would I? I was always right. I had to learn to be wrong.

Get to the why

Why go on a diet? I hate diets. I've never dieted in my life. I eat what I want. I have a great metabolism. I'm not fat. I'm just lovable. Why start now?

My wife's employers have a big Christmas party every year. It is my wife's one bargaining chip to get me to wear a suit. For her, I'll wear my nice black suit once a year.

I hadn't worn this suit in about a year. It fit then. It would fit now, right? With less than an hour before we were to leave for the party, I went into the bedroom to put on my nice suit. Yes, my wife picked out the tie. I did not argue. When I put the pants on, reality grabbed me by the waist. Literally. Those things would not fasten.

Suddenly, I understood why there were three, yes three, fasteners on these pants. There was an inside button that goes to the wide flap inside the pants zipper. Then there was the large metal hook at the waist. And finally, there was one more button on the outside at the waist.

It took me at least ten minutes to get button #1 to fasten. I was lying on my back on the bed like a commercial for skinny jeans. Once the first button was done, the other two took almost as long.

When I stood up, I was afraid to bend over or sit down. Dancing was definitely out of the question. If I had to go the restroom while we were there, the night was over. I felt like I was being slowly cut in two by some medieval torture device.

Three weeks later, I started a diet and exercise program. The next year, without any effort whatsoever, I put on those same pants in record time, took my wife to her party, and we danced. I suck at dancing, but so what?

Why indeed? It wasn't because she told me I needed to lose a few pounds. It was the pants that convinced me.

I had to look at my own life in detail and figure out what was driving my wife away from me. She could tell me. I begged her to tell me. Then, I had to shut up and see it for myself. See it in action.

I had to view my own life as something so out of shape that my marriage didn't fit anymore. Then, I had to do whatever it took to change that.

What I didn't do was tell my wife to "go on a diet" to fit the unyielding fabric that was our current way of life. I've noticed that when I take the first step in change, my wife sees and takes a step or two as well.

Big picture details

You get a much better view of things when you're on higher ground. Living in Colorado and spending time in the Rockies hiking and camping, you cannot avoid the views, the vistas, and the landscape. Come to think of it; you don't want to miss any of it.

However, with the amazing views, one can easily miss the little things right around you. You stand up for the big picture. You look around and focus on the little things to make a difference.

Big Picture: We're in the Colorado Rockies.

Little Picture: Is there enough room right here for our tent to fit?
Big Picture: Our marriage is getting along pretty well.
Little Picture: What can I do this week to make our marriage a little bit better?

Regardless of how good you feel your marriage is right now, chances are you're missing something. It may not be a big deal, but it can grow into one if unattended.

View every little thing you do for your spouse as one Lego brick added to your building project. You got it off the floor where you or she could step on it and scream. You added it to the big picture that is your marriage.

Never underestimate the power of doing something small that's part of the big picture. Every little thing counts.

Tweaking is a constant process

I own a red 1997 Jeep Wrangler, manual shift and all stock when I bought it. Now, anyone who owns a Wrangler has a tough time leaving it alone. By that, I mean leaving it in the original factory condition.

For years I kept it the same way I bought it. However, I had plans. After 12 years, it has an after-market front bumper and a winch. It has a new rear bumper and tire carrier. I've changed the style of the soft top, put on a lift, and am running 33" tires instead of the original 30" tires. I cut my fenders to accommodate the tires, and now I need new, wider, and prettier after-market fender flares. I could go on and on. You should see my roof rack.

Was my Jeep okay when I bought it? Sure. Probably. For several years I did nothing to it but drive it around. However, I wanted better. I wanted modifications. I wanted more capability. Because I wanted those things, I took action to get them.

When modifying a Jeep Wrangler, you need to know a few things.

First of all, the word Jeep stands for "Just Empty Every Pocket." Mods cost money. Last year I spent about $4,000 on upgrades. Yikes. (Yes, I did it with my wife's knowledge and blessing.) What I have now is a one-of-a-kind Jeep.

Modifying your marriage will come at a cost in time and effort—maybe even money. If you want a great marriage, you both have to work for it. I've noticed that when two people work together on a project, the outcome is much better than if just one did it.

Second, did I mention that my Jeep is one-of-a-kind? I did. My wife and I go off-roading with two other couples that also own Jeeps. Different years. Different colors. Different modifications. Different capabilities. Their Jeeps are one-of-a-kind as well. Dare I say that almost every Wrangler is different according to the owner's modifications and budget?

Your marriage is a one-of-a-kind arrangement. Don't compare it to your neighbor's, your sibling's, your parents', or anyone else's. Every marriage, to work for a lifetime, requires more than occasional adjustments. It will cost you time. It will require effort. It will cost you money, location, life direction, and sacrifice.

As soon as you start working on it together, you will have a once-in-a-lifetime, one-of-a-kind marriage like no other.

Is my Jeep perfect? Far from it. My headlights don't work when it's cold outside. I have no idea why. It doesn't matter, because I love my Jeep. I'll just keep working on it.

Is my marriage perfect? Far from it. She buys too many shoes. It's an issue. I don't care, because I have a marriage that I'm constantly working on, and so does my wife.

So, get at it. Take the first step. Build your marriage. Modify. Work at it. The payoff far exceeds any expense.

I know. I almost lost her. Then I did something about it.

One Final Note

It's the little things that add up. I began to do little things that took only one or two minutes. I did them for my wife.

Little things can add up quickly like compound interest. Just keep doing them. Husbands do little things for their wives. Wives do little things for their husband. Nothing is expected in return. Do them for as long as it takes.

Here's a final quick list of the little things

- Pour the bath water
- Clean up the kitchen
- Give spontaneous hugs.
- Hold the door.
- Carry the bag.
- Keep your mouth shut.
- Voice zero criticism.
- Smile.
- Make the bed.
- Wave goodbye.
- Argue nicely.
- Laugh with each other.
- Apologize when you're wrong.
- Take the first step to make up.
- Never yell at him/her.
- Talk to each other about everything.
- Shut up and listen.
- Accept their style of dress.
- Share the load with finances.

- Spend less, regardless.
- Exercise together.
- Hold hands.
- Support each other's hobbies.
- Pray for each other.
- Pray with each other.
- Surprise him/her.
- Never force an issue. Talk through an issue.
- Opinions are exactly that: Opinions.
- Be protective of each other, instead of being jealous.
- Listen to your intuition about each other. Share it.
- Be the first to encourage.
- Be the last to discourage.
- Never say, "I told you so."
- Did I mention hugging?
- Do the unexpected chore.
- Send a text just to say "I Love You."
- Give a well-timed, inexpensive gift.
- Clean something you don't normally clean.
- Book a room. Go there together.
- Stop being a backseat driver.
- Let them know you trust them. Then trust them.
- Cry with each other.
- Celebrate with each other.
- Run away together.
- A kiss a day no matter what.

ABOUT THE AUTHOR

Bill McConnell is a husband, father, speaker, author and coach. He spent 23 years in local church staff ministry. He has been a program coordinator for collaborative care management with a regional hospital. He is a certified Project Manager. Hiking, camping, 4-wheeling, and tweaking the Jeep are things that get him away from a computer.

His amazing wife, Lisa, is a Family Nurse Practitioner serving as a solo provider in a family practice clinic. She also does occasional work at an Urgent Care Unit, as well as optional work as an FNP staffing the campus clinic at a Division 1 university. Yeah, she's "Type A" amazing.

Together they have one daughter, Shelby, a former missionary in Guatemala and current site director with the Boys & Girls Club. She has a pet rabbit named "Hazel Rah." They both live in the basement, and her parents are okay with that.

The family dog, Ziggi, is a purebred Aussie (with a tail) who as you already know, only sheds two times per year.

GOOD BOOKS NEED
GOOD BOOK REVIEWS

Success after reading a book like this is a couple having a better marriage and a better understanding of themselves and each other. I hope I've accomplished that in this book.

Before you toss this on the shelf, I'd like to thank you for buying it and reading it.

You could have picked from dozens of books on marriage and relationships, yet you took a chance and bought this one.

Now I'd like to ask for a small favor. Could you please take a minute or two and leave an honest review for this book on Amazon?

This feedback will help me develop future resources and tools related to my focus on my speaking, writing and future projects. I cannot do it better without your input.

Thank you!